# Shakespeare Country

# ALSO BY SUSAN HILL

# Shakespeare Country

## Susan Hill

with photographs by Rob Talbot
in association with Robin Whiteman

MICHAEL JOSEPH – LONDON

For my husband
Stanley Wells
the *real* Shakespearean

# Contents

First published in Great Britain by
Michael Joseph Limited
27 Wrights Lane, London W8
1987

British Library Cataloguing in Publication Data
Hill, Susan, 1942–
    Shakespeare Country.
    1. Warwickshire—Description and travel
    I. Title
    914.24'804858     DA670.W3

    ISBN 0-7181-2738-2

Printed and bound in the Netherlands by
Royal Smeets Offset B.V. Weert.

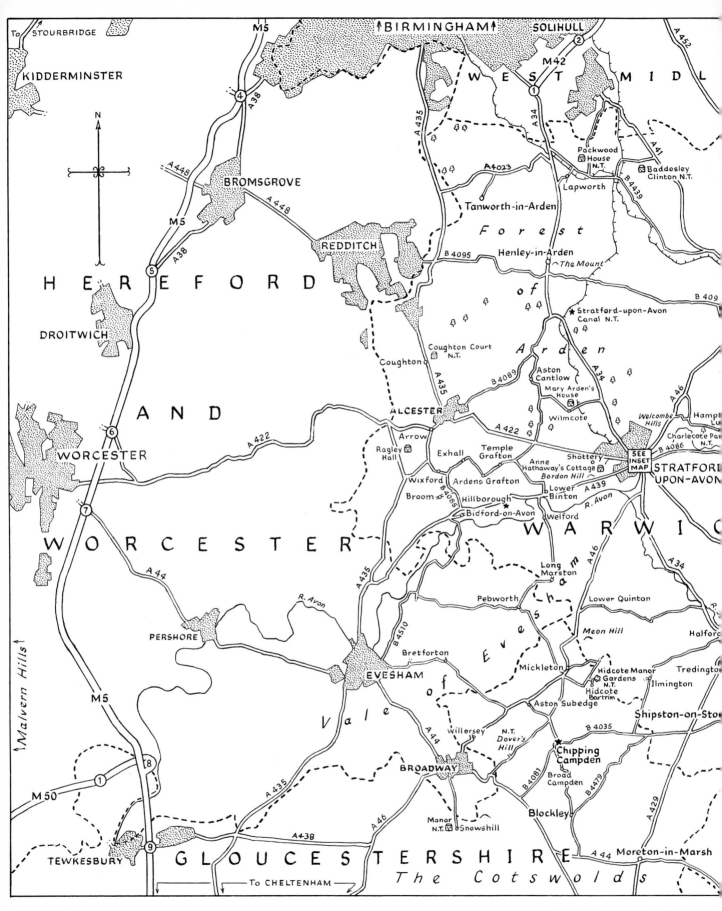

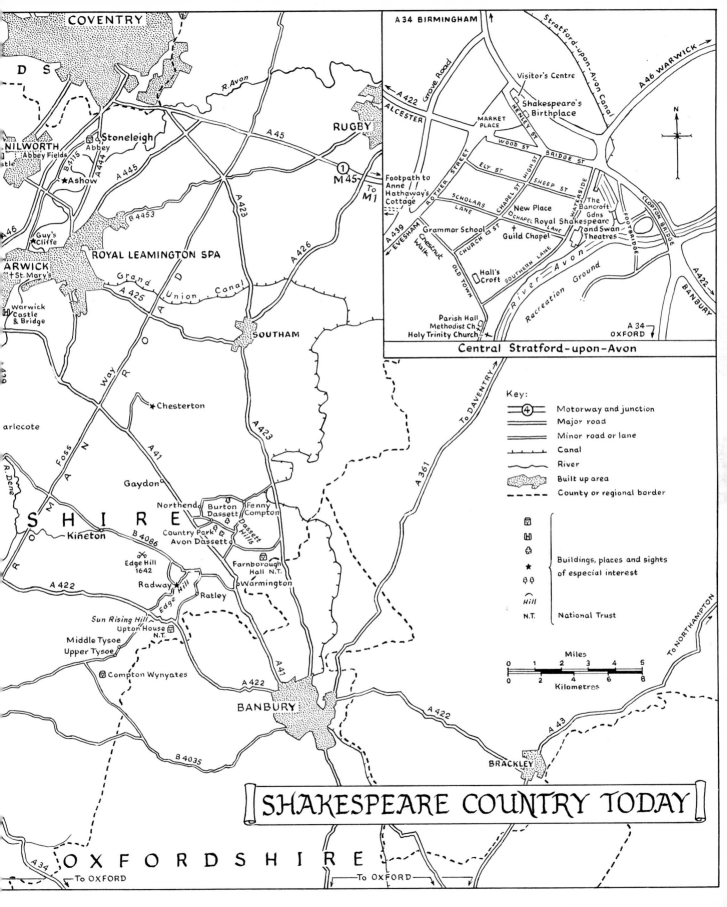

**COVENTRY**

D S

KENILWORTH
Abbey Fields
Castle
Stoneleigh
Abbey
Ashow
B 4115
A 444
A 445
B 4453
R. Avon
A 45
RUGBY
M 45
①
To M1

Guy's Cliffe
WARWICK
St. Mary's
Warwick Castle & Bridge
A 46
ROYAL LEAMINGTON SPA
Grand Union Canal
A 425
FOSS WAY ROMAN
A 423
A 426
SOUTHAM

Chesterton
A 423

arlcote

S H I R E
R. Dene
A 422
FOSS WAY ROMAN
A 41
Gaydon
Northend
Burton Dassett
Fenny Compton
Country Park
Avon Dassett
Dassett Hills

Kineton
B 4086
Edge Hill 1642
Radway
Edge Hill
Ratley
Farnborough Hall N.T.
Warmington

Sun Rising Hill
Upton House N.T.
Middle Tysoe
Upper Tysoe
Compton Wynyates
A 422
A 41
A 361
To DAVENTRY

B 4035
BANBURY
A 422
A 422
A 43
BRACKLEY

To NORTHAMPTON

### Central Stratford-upon-Avon

A 34 BIRMINGHAM
Stratford-upon-Avon Canal
A 46 WARWICK
A 422
ALCESTER
Grove Road
Visitor's Centre
Shakespeare's Birthplace
Henley St
Market Place
Wood St
Bridge St
Ely St
High St
Sheep St
Rother Street
Scholars Lane
Chapel St
New Place
Chapel Lane
Royal Shakespeare and Swan Theatres
The Bancroft Gdns
Waterside
Clopton Bridge
Footpath to Anne Hathaway's Cottage
A 439 EVESHAM
Chestnut Walk
Grammar School
Church St
Guild Chapel
Hall's Croft
Old Town
Southern Lane
River Avon
Recreation Ground
Parish Hall
Methodist Ch.
Holy Trinity Church
A 422 BANBURY
A 34 OXFORD
N

### Key:

| | |
|---|---|
| ④ | Motorway and junction |
| | Major road |
| | Minor road or lane |
| | Canal |
| | River |
| | Built up area |
| | County or regional border |

Buildings, places and sights of especial interest

*Hill*

N.T. — National Trust

Miles
0 1 2 3 4 5
Kilometres
0 2 4 6 8

# SHAKESPEARE COUNTRY TODAY

**OXFORDSHIRE**

A 34
To OXFORD
To OXFORD

# Introduction

The January day in 1958 on which my father came home and announced that we were moving from Yorkshire to the Midlands might well have been a bitter one indeed. I was sixteen. I had been born in Scarborough, that dramatic, handsome town, set on cliffs overlooking the cold North Sea, and had scarcely been outside the county, my roots were firmly embedded there. But I was beginning to be restless, to look to the world outside, and dream dreams about it, see the far horizons; the place, now that adulthood was approaching, seemed suddenly parochial, dated, dull. I was reading a lot, and books told me about a different kind of life. I was also beginning to have a passion, fostered by my mother, for all things theatrical, and to discover and be excited by Shakespeare.

So instead of feeling threatened or fearful at the prospect of such a profound change in my life, I felt only a great uprush of glee, and went to the drawer and took out the pre-war Michelin map of England that my father had used to plan cycling tours, as a young man. I can see it now, spread out over the Turkey-red carpet, a rough-textured map with cotton backing and dark lines down the seams where it had been folded and re-folded so many times. I traced the

(Previous page) *Ridge-and-furrow on Meon Hill, near Ilmington.* (Below and right) *The River Avon near Stratford*

old pink 'A' road with my finger, down from the north to Warwickshire, and the city of Coventry, where we were to live. But the place I was looking for lay directly south of there. *Stratford-upon-Avon*. Found it. 'How far?' 'Not far at all. Fifteen miles?' I stared and stared at the name of the town, and at those around it, Warwick, Kenilworth, Henley-in-Arden, real places, near to which I would be living, and which I could visit soon. Yet places from another world, too, another landscape, an imaginary one, the playwright's own, about which I was now always reading.

Although nowadays, in middle age, my dreams and memories are all of the sea and of my early Yorkshire childhood, the beaches, the buildings, the cliffs and gardens and countryside around, and although it seems closer to me, and even more significant, and more vivid, the further away I go from it in time, when I actually left it I cast it off thankfully, like a chrysalis, turned my back and paid it no more heed. My head was full of the Forest of Arden, the Swan of Avon, and the Earls of Warwick, the great families of Charlecote and Coughton and Packwood. I read of Leofric and Lady Godiva, and the burning of Coventry Cathedral, dreamed of Hamlet and Horatio, Oberon and Titania, Rosalind and Orlando. I borrowed old-fashioned travel books from the library, with titles like *Rambles in Shakespeare Land* and *Through the Heart of England*.

My first impression of the county which was to be my home for the next twenty-five years, and in which so much of importance was to happen to me, was already formed before I had set foot in it. I had that imaginary vision, gleaned from guide books and English literature, postcards, maps and paintings, which always helps to form one's idea of a place in advance and which to some extent overlays and colours the reality forever after. A host of associations, literary, historical, theatrical, romantic, already accrued to my vision of the Shakespeare country, and so many others have

been added since that perhaps I have never seen what it actually looks like, clearly and simply. And now there are memories like encrustations, so that whenever I am in that countryside, walking about those places, what I see is inextricably bound up with what I feel and remember about my own past there. But this is the way that places become more than places, become part of oneself and fill the heart, that is why they are so often more than the sum of their visible, tangible, recordable elements.

As soon as I possibly could, after our arrival in Coventry, I took the red bus out of it again. It was a spring Saturday, one of those rare, perfect days in May. I was spending my own pocket money and insisted on going alone, which seemed a bolder gesture then than it would now, but I had never travelled about in a strange part of the country by myself before, and scarcely even knew my way down to the bus station; a tame adventure perhaps, but an adventure nevertheless, to a sheltered and green sixteen year old, fresh from Yorkshire.

When I found the right bus, and saw its sign – X90, Stratford-upon-Avon – my heart leaped; when I climbed up onto the top deck and made my way right to the very front, I had a sense of dazed unreality, of absolute disbelief.

It was the best of all possible ways to make that journey, see that countryside, enter Stratford for the very first time. The road is different now, a fast dual carriageway cutting directly through the open fields, by-passing all the villages and market towns; it is an efficient, boring road. But then the bus ground its slow way through Kenilworth and Warwick and all stops between, past the chestnut and sycamore trees, the oaks, and the beeches, whose branches kept scraping the bus roof above my head. I looked down upon tiles and thatch, into the green hearts of the trees, across the sloping fields full of spring barley. It was all quite unlike the bleak, bare North Yorkshire moors that I was used to, this gentle, restful, quietly

*Early morning*

beautiful, leafy, undulating county, softer, mellower, lusher than anything I knew, and tamer, too. But after those years of wild and windswept scenery, this was what I wanted.

The bus journey took a magic hour, but journey's end was what I looked for – my first and dazzling sight of the streets, the river, the theatre, the church spire, of Stratford.

I have had the same feeling occasionally at other times in my life – when I first trod the shingle beach at Aldeburgh, or came out of an unremarkable railway station building and saw the city of Venice, reflected in water at my feet – but because of my youth and naivety, my gladness, hope for the future and sense of daring, all coming together in the warm spring sunshine that sparkled on the Avon, where the swans glided, puffed and white as meringues, because of all that, perhaps I have never felt quite as I did that day.

And so I came to the Shakespeare country. Apart from three years in London, at university, I was to stay there. During the years that followed, I made the same journey on the top deck of the Midland Red bus many times, and travelled, by bicycle, on foot, and later by car, in other directions too, getting to know the lanes and villages and market towns, the fields and low hills and all the ramifications of river and canal that mesh the county. I learned the broad outline and the minute detail of so much, and so much became important.

One Maundy Thursday in the early 1960s, I was driven out in a dashing, open-topped car to Lower Quinton, and Ilmington, to Mickleton and finally, Chipping Campden, for lunch, by a man who was to change my life. On this April day, the countryside was on the very brink of spring and I on the brink of love, and I recall everything about the journey in that vivid, acute way we do remember scenes and times when they have been charged with intense emotion. The first sight of the curve of honey-coloured stone houses leading into the wide main street of Campden is a greatly pleasing one and apart from the bright tin ribbon of cars now always winding along each side of it, it is one that cannot have changed very much since the fifteenth century.

So many vistas and views, buildings and monuments in one's own even quite recent past have changed almost out of recognition when revisited, things knocked down and things gone up, widened or narrowed, ploughed or built over, it is sometimes like having one's own limbs lopped off when such drastic change affects places one cares about. But much of the Shakespeare country is, at least at heart and in essence, much the same as it has been for hundreds of years. Certainly, I can go back into that part of my own past that belongs there and still find my way around.

I lived for a long time in the Heart of England and, in truth, have never completely left it – and we have a house in Stratford now – but I have never written about it, in fiction or even in fact (apart from setting an early novel, *Gentleman and Ladies*, in a heavily modified Chipping Campden). For this has become a *real* country to me, where my own real life has been lived, it is no longer the stuff of the imagination.

In 1968, I moved to Leamington Spa. I liked its broad, tree-lined avenues and spacious Italianate villas and stuccoed Regency crescents, its elegant shopping streets and pretty public gardens, the ducks and canoes on its river. From there I roved out and about in a battered van, driving to north, south, east and west of the county and beyond it, often early in the morning or very late at night, learning the place and taking it all rather for granted, as one does with comfortable, familiar, everyday surroundings.

I went away from Warwickshire a lot in those days, too, months of the winter to a North-Sea-facing house in Suffolk, months of the summer to a cottage buried below the Dorset downs, to find solitude and working space and landscapes of the inner eye, and write of them. But the road always led home to the Shakespeare country, and in the end, back to the heart of it, to Stratford where it all began, and marriage and my family, happiness.

I have often wondered, when I have thought about the ways in which it has and has not changed in my time, how Shakespeare himself might see his own country now, what he would have a good chance of recognising, and what would be utterly strange. All the trappings of modern life would be foreign to him, of course, and transport and, most of all, the changes the internal combustion engine has wrought. There are far fewer trees now, too. In his time, the Forest of Arden covered the county like a dense dark animal pelt, barring the way to invaders and making travel difficult and dangerous. Since my own early years there, the death of the elm has been the greatest single factor in the alteration of the landscape, whole vistas have been altered, laid bare, spoilt. But there *are* still a great many trees; drive through the lanes, look out across the farmland, and you see innumerable small copses, patches of broadleaf woodland, limes, great spreading oaks under which the cattle and sheep gather in the heat of the day. There are chestnuts along many a Stratford street and poplars in its public gardens, osiers and willows along the river bank; this is still leafy Warwickshire.

Villages have grown outwards, new houses spreading like stains over the surrounding fields; towns that were small are now big, great houses that once stood alone are now too close for comfort to busy highways. And there are many, many more people, living and working, and most of all, visiting.

And yet, of all the flowers and birds, trees and creatures mentioned in Shakespeare's plays, most may easily be found today. Cottage gardens abound. Farming is mechanised, crops are new, yet the farmer still grows wheat and barley, keeps pigs, cows, sheep and hens, sows the seed and cuts the hay and brings home the harvest.

Of all the tradesmen mentioned in the Shakespeare canon, there may no longer be ostlers and butter-women, bellows-menders and whittawers, swineherds or gallows-men at work in town and country, but there are the butcher and the baker and the fruiterer, the

*Sheep at sunset*

inn-keeper and the thatcher, gardener and smith, lawyer, doctor and clerk, and even, in Ilmington, the hurdle-maker. There is still a beadle in Stratford, and plenty of morris men on high days and holidays, dancing the ancient dances to the old tunes, and now, as then, the actors; there is still buying and selling on market day, working in the fields and woods, hunting, fishing, shooting, milking, riding, the burgeoning of the trees in spring and the shortest days 'when blood be nipped and ways be foul', there are christenings and burials, merrymaking and marriages. Much of life goes on in the way it always did.

There are houses left, both castles and cottages, which Shakespeare would have known, and if the roads north to Coventry and south to London would seem quite different to him, the signposts still do point to those cities, and the same journey can be undertaken.

The plays are dyed in and shot through with the life and atmosphere, the language and landscape of his

countryside. Reading *As You Like It*, or *Love's Labour's Lost* or the history plays, you gain a tremendously strong sense of how it was, how it looked, smelled, sounded. Yet it is all interwoven in tiny details, into the main dramatic body of the work; when you try to extract those long passages you think you remember, describing Elizabethan England, and Warwickshire, town and village life, you cannot find them after all, they are not there. Images of birds, and flowers in gardens, mention of dawn and dusk, of spider and beetle and dipper, hare and hounds, tapster and blacksmith, passing mentions of how this branch bent or that wind blew, these you will find, and realise from it all that here was a man who had *observed*, all his life, knew the ways of the countryside in which he grew up, the lie of the land, the smell and feel and heat and cold of it, as well as he knew himself, in an everyday, intimately familiar way. The plays are not descriptive, as novels would be, just because they *are* plays, dramas about human events and emotions. You catch the landscape of them incidentally, as it were, and yet it is all of a piece with the rest; you breathe in the Shakespeare country as you read or listen. Just as, when you go there now and wander about, whether through the

*Fields of oilseed rape and buttercups near Snitterfield*

streets of Stratford, in and out of all those famous houses, or further afield, in among the little villages, or about the parks and gardens, battlements and great halls of grand Elizabethan and medieval buildings, you can see, hear, sense, Shakespeare the man, and Shakespeare's writings, and the life of his town and countryside, all about you.

Even today.

*The Fleece Inn at Bretforton*

'*The National Trust acquired the Fleece in 1978 when it was bequeathed to them by Miss Lola Taplin, whose family had owned it for generations. The medieval building was a farm until converted into a beerhouse in 1848. In those days, the pub had its own brewery and all three parlours were served from one hatch in the hall.*

'*Ale was stored in casks away from the bars to keep it cool and this is the origin of the "taprooms" found in many Victorian pubs. The original system has given way to hand pumps, but apart from a serving bar near the hatch, the whole of the interior has changed little over the years.*

'*When the pub was given to the National Trust, all the furnishings were included and there are many antiques; particularly fine is a forty-eight piece set of Stuart pewter.'*

*From* English Country Pubs *by Derry Brabbs (Weidenfeld & Nicolson, 1986)*

# Stratford-upon-Avon

Famous people do seem to have made a habit of being born in pretty places – Mozart in Salzburg, Wordsworth in the Lake District, Hardy in Dorset, the Brontës in Yorkshire. It all helps to establish them as focuses for visitors, but those visitors would still come, simply to enjoy the charms of the locality. And Stratford's charms are very evident.

There is, and always has been, far more to the town than William Shakespeare. Take away the Shakespeare connection and it would certainly not sink into decay and oblivion as would, say, Venice, without the tourists which are now its life-blood. Stratford would have fewer visitors, of course, particularly from overseas, and suffer a considerable loss of income and employment from the tourist industry. Without Shakespeare, there would be no theatre, no actors – it would be a very different place, but perhaps only superficially. It would continue to flourish as the market town serving a wide area, as it has since the twelfth century. Light industry is here, too. Stratford always feels to me a Midlands town rather than one belonging to rural, southern England, on whose borders it stands. Its local accent is a modified Birmingham one, it is not far from the Black Country, and it has long had satellite industries serving the motor trade, though since the 1970s, it has suffered from the general economic decline of West Midlands engineering, and many of the small factories that once employed so many, no longer exist. It is becoming more of a general commercial, less of a manufacturing town.

A great many people live and work here who have nothing at all to do with Shakespeare or tourism, and if you stay in the town long enough, and especially out of season, you discover that at heart it is they who predominate, their lives and tastes shape the place now, and you realise that tourism is really only a superficial, though very prominent and lucrative, icing on the cake.

Walk through the main streets on any Saturday

morning, and the majority of people you will see are locals doing their shopping, weaving an expert path to butcher, baker and candlestick-maker through Japanese photographing the exterior of the Shakespeare Hotel and Americans in tartan trousers buying tartan trousers.

Go down onto the Bancroft gardens on any summer Sunday afternoon and you will see mainly English families at play – picnicking, sleeping, throwing Frisbees, watching the boats go by, though in amongst them there will certainly be Swedes with haversacks and crocodiles of teenagers from France. It has never struck me as a cosmopolitan place. Nor does it have an immigrant community – a surprising fact, when you know how large a proportion of the West Midlands population is Asian or Afro-Caribbean.

Stratford is an English town and, on the whole, working rather than middle class, straightforward rather than genteel, though it has its select side. And it has a lot in common with many another English town set beside a river, with Henley-on-Thames or Maidenhead, Hereford or Ross-on-Wye.

Its basic, central plan is very simple – it is rather difficult to get seriously lost in Stratford – and unchanged since the Middle Ages. Three streets run parallel to the river, crossed by three streets at right angles to it. Otherwise, like any similar place, it spreads out, with houses lining the leafy roads, leading north, south, east and west, raw, red estates creeping over the fields, and plenty of corrugated warehouses.

But in the centre, all is easy walking, and very compact, and with a pleasing sight – a half-timbered house, a sudden glimpse of the river, a church, a green sward – on every corner.

I don't know many places where I get so much delight from simply strolling about. It's a floral town, too, not only in the pride of civic hanging baskets and official window-boxes, but in the large number of beautiful private gardens, cottage gardens in the finest English sense, brought to town. Go down the long narrow streets of Old Town, the area in front of Holy Trinity Church, and see the roses and clematis and

(Previous page) *Shakespeare's Birthplace*

*The River Avon at Guy's Cliffe*

honeysuckle clambering over every wall, the plant pots and tubs and boxes and upturned buckets overflowing with flowers at every front door, the sight of bright beds and borders at the bottom of alleyways, the proliferation of trees and shrubs crowded into a few acres.

It's a curious place in which to live. In the summer, you go out to do your shopping as early as possible, and rush home to avoid the crowds, the jams, the noise; and sometimes, on a hot Bank Holiday, if you're feeling paranoid, it seems as if every nook and cranny of the place, and your own very back yard, might be invaded by visitors. But they won't be. Turn a corner away from the main tourist route, and all is quiet, there are only neighbours.

And very early in the morning, or after six o'clock in the evening, the place is half-empty wherever you go, airy, leafy, and it is a pleasure to be out; though sometimes, on a hot summer's night, the crowds spilling out of the theatre and strolling back to cars and coaches and hotels, the open doors of cafés and pubs from which come the smells of food and wine, and the sounds of conviviality, can give it all a slightly raffish, continental air which has its own kind of fleeting charm.

In late autumn, the atmosphere changes again, as the nights draw in and the last of the coaches roll away, and landladies close their B and Bs and fly off to Tenerife. Then, the Christmas tree goes up on the green island at the top of Bridge Street where, hundreds of years ago, the market was, and the Christmas lights come on all over the town – and Stratford is rightly proud of its Christmas lights. People you haven't seen all season come out of retreat, and find they can talk to one another quite comfortably again, across the width of the street, and the amateur operatic society takes over the theatre where Shakespeare used to be.

I like it best in winter, when the trees are bare and the river may even freeze over and dawn is breathtakingly beautiful, and lights from all the little shops and houses – for it *is* a little, a small-scale, a low-lying, town – are friendly, though the fogs come chill from off the water and the wind can whistle down the streets like a train through a tunnel.

But you can breathe in Stratford then, have space and time to learn the side of it that the visitors, especially those who only gaze at it through the tinted windows of air-conditioned coaches, never see.

*Shakespeare's Birthplace. On 23 April 1552, John, father of William Shakespeare, is on record as having paid a fine of one shilling for allowing an unauthorised midden – or muck-heap – to stand outside his house in Henley Street, Stratford, almost certainly the house in which the playwright was born and which is now one of the most visited literary shrines in the world.*

*In Shakespeare's day, there were in fact two houses there, bought at separate dates, but these were later joined to form what is now one long, very imposing, three-gabled house.*

*On his father's death, it passed to William Shakespeare, and then remained in the family until the nineteenth century when it became first a butcher's shop, before being pur-chased on behalf of the nation as a public trust, in 1847.*

*In less sensitive and law-abiding times, many visitors carved their names on the windows and plaster walls of the traditional birth-room (below) and they can still be seen today – though whether Sir Walter Scott, Tennyson, Dickens and the actor Edmund Kean engraved their own signatures, or had their names taken in vain, is a moot point.*

*The house has also inspired some charming descriptions, including one by the historian Edgar Fripp: 'Shadows and weird noises are in the rafters, the wind is in the chimneys, crickets are on the hearth, fairies glisten in the light of the dying fire, through leaded windows shines the moon, without is the tu-whit to-whoo of the loved brown owl.'*

It's a truism that people who live in famous places rarely visit the tourist sites. Brighton Pavilion is not full of Brightonians, nor Blenheim with the residents of Woodstock, and a good many Londoners will have lived all their lives in the metropolis and never been to the Tower.

It was Shakespeare who originally drew me to Stratford, as he draws thousands every year, but the Shakespeare of the plays, the theatre where they were performed and the actors who inhabited it, not the burgher of Stratford. In those early years, I came as often as I could afford to on the red bus, to queue for standing tickets, but I didn't go near the Birthplace – I'm not even sure that I knew it existed, and Anne Hathaway's Cottage was only a familiar picture on a biscuit tin.

Indeed, when I came to live in the town, and married, as it were, into Shakespeare, I still didn't visit the properties for a long while, and when I eventually did, it was by accident, and because they were part of everyday life, rather than for any Shakespeare association. I met friends for lunch or tea in the garden of Hall's Croft, and the biennial Shakespeare Conference, of which my husband was the Secretary, holds its garden party there; when my elder daughter was a baby, I pushed her pram into the great garden of New Place, and sat on a bench to read while she slept peacefully beneath the mighty beech tree that used to stand so handsomely there – before it had to be felled, for safety's sake.

I first went through the Birthplace when dutifully taking part in my first Birthday Celebration procession, and it was on a visit to a garden centre to buy a magnolia tree, one dismal November afternoon, that I passed by Anne Hathaway's Cottage and thought to stop there. It was quite deserted, the garden bleak, with bare earth and the trees dripping, and the floorboards of the dark little house echoed only to my own footsteps.

*New Place and its garden*

Yet the more I think about it, the more strongly I feel that this is the best, the only satisfactory way, to discover Shakespeare's town and the houses connected with him, and to a large extent it's a way open only to those who live in or near there, or at least, who come to stay for a period, as the theatre people do. Only in this way can the feel, the sense, the *spirit*, of the houses creep up on you, only this way, by simply getting on with everyday life in Stratford-upon-Avon as it is now can you begin to imagine how it might have been. You have to come at it from the wrong end, rather as Alice discovered, in *Through the Looking Glass*, that the only way to get up the path to the front door of the house was to turn her back on it and walk away in the opposite direction.

Join a queue, march into the Shakespeare properties through the front door, in a crowd, determine to understand how it all was then, capture the authentic atmosphere, and it will evade you and slip through your fingers, you will get nothing at all. I have heard people who have visited the Holy Land say the same; they have toured the sites wearily, the place of Christ's Nativity, the Garden of Gethsemane – nothing. But they have gone out in the country around, sat by the shores of the Lake of Galilee in the cool of the early morning, broken bread, and then . . .

Even if you know a good deal of Elizabethan history, and have a vivid imagination, it is hardest of all to get any sense of the past in and around the actual Birthplace, or to convince yourself that this is somewhere Shakespeare himself may have been.

On one side is the thundering roar of heavy lorry traffic tearing up the Birmingham Road; on the other, busy, noisy little Henley Street, with its Souvenirs of Wales, and replica shops selling models of London policemen, its library, fishmonger, Chinese restaurant, supermarket. And if the shop fronts are incongruous, so are most of the houses themselves, for they are eighteenth-century buildings. Even when you see half-timbering, do not imagine you are seeing what Shakespeare saw. It was the Victorians who uncovered the wood on the façades of old houses – in the sixteenth century they were covered over with plaster and board. It looks nicer now, in all probability, but not as it originally was.

In order to stagger the large crowds, the entrance to Shakespeare's Birthplace begins in the Visitors' Centre which dominates the top end of Henley Street, uncompromisingly modern, and through whose curiously dead-seeming foyers one has to pass; but then, out into the garden – and one of the principal joys of all the properties are the gardens, meticulously planted and tended, full of interest and delight. Whether or not it was all as neat and bright and quaint as this in the sixteenth century we do not know, though the Elizabethans were certainly serious gardeners.

And so, through a low doorway, into the little house itself, where everything is polished and gleaming and spotless, immaculately cared for. Would it have been? But the question is irrelevant, for this is a museum, not a living house. Such places always are. The furniture is in period, but it was brought here during the nineteenth century; there is an exhibition on the walls, there are enthusiastic guides and polite notices. What also always strikes me about these interiors is that they

*An eglantine rose in the garden of New Place*

all seem somehow interchangeable; close your eyes in the Birthplace, open them again and, quite easily, you could have been transported to Anne Hathaway's Cottage.

And how authentic *are* the houses? If this is the Birthplace, *is* it the Birthplace? Well yes, very probably, the documentary evidence for it is stronger than for most of the others, except for New Place – the house that is no longer there at all! Otherwise, tradition plays a major part. In the case of Hall's Croft, it is a very late tradition indeed, reaching back only as far as the nineteenth century, when there is the first record that the house was so named. Before then, it was called Cambridge House and was a girls' school. *Tradition* has it that Shakespeare's daughter, Susanna, lived there with her husband, John Hall, but there is no *evidence*.

We know that Shakespeare married Anne Hathaway, who came from the village of Shottery, and that the house now known as Anne Hathaway's Cottage was in possession of the Hathaway family in later centuries. They were unlikely to have moved from some other (now vanished) farm in the same village – people did not move so casually then as they do now, and properties were handed down within the family. All the same, we cannot be absolutely certain about the cottage, any, more than we can about the house now known as Mary Arden's, at Wilmcote. We know that Shakespeare's mother came from there, and that her family was a prosperous one, and owned a large property. Tradition has it that this is the farmhouse in which she had lived. We cannot be certain.

*Hall's Croft*

But really – so what? Some people *do* want certainty, the *frisson* that comes from being in the actual place, on the very spot. They are the ones whose pilgrimage to the Holy Land depends so much on faith in the authenticity of the sacred places. 'This is the spot where stood the stable in which Jesus Christ was born, and I am here, and so it must be true.'

But I am not such a believer, and it is not in such a way that I get my own intimations of Shakespeare.

Those come on the wind, and all unexpectedly – when I am looking at the river from the terrace of the churchyard on a cold winter's afternoon, standing in the orchard at Anne Hathaway's on a quiet Sunday morning in April, among the blossoms and the first bees, or in the cool, dark, ancient dovecote, at Mary Arden's House – ordinary places, everyday moments, when the centuries suddenly seem to touch, with no time in between. Then, I feel that he might be around the next corner, just out of sight, watching, listening, that in just such a place, on just such a day, he could have come here.

*Hall's Croft.* (Opposite top) *The Hall and* (opposite bottom) *the bedroom.* (Below) *The garden*

The pleasure of the properties lies, for me, not in their historical authenticity, but simply in their individual and particular charm, setting, atmosphere. Certainly, when you visit them, you may learn a considerable amount about the domestic architecture and accoutrements of provincial Elizabethan life, and you may even come away with some faint idea of Stratford in Shakespeare's time. And if you are a pilgrim, then the journey itself, and the fact of your having been there are all that will matter to you.

But go there open-minded, without prejudice or expectation, go when it is quieter, in drizzly autumn or January snow, go late on a Wednesday afternoon, or first thing on Sunday morning out of the summer season, and linger, do not rush, and perhaps you will get something more – and infinitely more precious.

Besides, for many, it is the houses themselves, not the man, which matter. And Hall's Croft, which has the most tenuous of Shakespeare connections, is my own particular favourite, and most of all, at half past four on a sunny summer afternoon. The house is an oasis, cool and dark, stone-flagged, wonderfully welcoming on a hot day. There are always jugs and bowls of fresh flowers on the oak tables and dressers, and never too many visitors at once. It smells of lavender and Brasso. At the far end of the hall, you go through the low door and out into the brightness of one of the best of all the gardens, completely enclosed by high walls, and with a fine green sward, finely mown, that leads with a bit of a flourish up to a rather theatrical terrace at the far end. A gnarled and ancient mulberry

(Below and opposite) *Mary Arden's house at Wilmcote;* (opposite bottom) *the kitchen*

tree, propped up by iron supports, graces the grass. It looks dead, but it is not. In August, my children sit under it, and wait for the fruit to fall, and squash them between their little fingers until the purple juice oozes deliciously, messily out. The smell and the sharp taste of mulberry juice, warmed by the late summer sun, is one of the joys of a Stratford summer.

Along the eastern edge of the garden, a line of poplars, always rustling, never still, even on the stillest of days, casts long, long shadows. There are canvas chairs dotted here and there about the grass. Old men asleep under panama hats. And that most English of sounds, the chink of spoon against teacup, and cup against saucer, afternoon tea in the garden. To sit here, eyes half-closed, listening to the leaves and the bees buzzing in the lavender bushes that tumble over the wall, is to be very content.

And the second best joy of a summer's afternoon is to visit Mary Arden's House, at Wilmcote, a couple of miles outside Stratford, and never mind whether it really was or not. It has an atmosphere and a tranquillity about it which are unique among the Shakespeare properties; the old walls look buttery in the sunshine, the green courtyard and the grey cobblestones, the grainy wood of the barn beams, the dark and coolth of the dovecote, all blend together, feel completely harmonious.

*Mary Arden's house, reputed to have belonged to Shakespeare's mother's family, was occupied as a working farmhouse until this century, and this has ensured its preservation in its original condition, at least so far as the structure and arrangement of the rooms and outbuildings.*

*In the kitchen* (previous page), *the great open fireplace remains intact, though the baking-oven next to it has disappeared; it has a fine stone-flagged floor and a raftered ceiling. So does the great hall* (below left), *and in these rooms now, farmhouse furniture is displayed, all neatly, cleanly arranged, rather more as in a museum of country life than a working kitchen. But in spite of the tidiness, the spit and the polish, something of a farmhouse atmosphere seeps through.*

*Anne Hathaway's cottage*

You *can* encounter crowds here, but only relatively speaking – even in August, the numbers of people making the journey out from Stratford are never too great at any one time, though during weekdays of the school summer term, you may well find yourself among hordes of assorted children with the ubiquitous clipboards, buzzing about the place, intent upon gathering information for a project. It's the best and nicest house for them to visit, there is fresh air to breathe and space for them to spill out into, and a great many things to look at, find out about, write about. Perhaps they do come under duress, but I bet their memories of it are happy.

Mary Arden's House is actually a complex of build-ings, including the Glebe Farm, bought and restored in recent years, as well as outbuildings, barns, lawns, gardens. Glebe Farm has nothing to do with Shakespeare, or with Elizabethan England; it is set out as a model-cum-exhibition of how it would have been, rather idealistically speaking, in the nineteenth century, all pretty, tidy, neat. Never mind, it's all extremely pleasant. So are the open spaces in between Mary Arden's House and Glebe Farm, and the path across the grassy meadow, and the old fashioned cottage garden and the vegetable patch and the pigsty. Everything is visually of a piece. You can wander in and out of the courtyard and lawns and the plain, big barn, as well as go into the house that may, perhaps, possibly, have belonged to Shakespeare's mother's family.

It all seems delightfully informal and homely, there are not so many bossy notices as usual and children don't feel restricted. There are such lovely stone walls, such handsome great trees, such buttercups-and-daisies. In those days, rather than these days, it wouldn't have been so tidy, and there would have been some hens scritch-scratching about, as well as a pig in the sty, and the outlook would have been even more open, without the surrounding, modern houses of Wilmcote village within sight. You were out in real country then, a long walk or ride from Stratford Town. But the doves would have cooed in the high, dark dovecote and the bees droned in and out of the foxgloves and perhaps a marmalade cat would have sat on the step in the sun, just as I saw it one day. Unless it was only the ghost of a cat. And at night, owls in the trees. The same creatures of the poems and plays, of the man who must certainly, almost certainly, have come here, four hundred years or so ago.

But there are joys at other times of the year. Shottery was once a cluster of farmhouses, on the very edge of the Forest of Arden. Shakespeare walked across fields to woo Anne Hathaway there. Now, as Sam Schoenbaum puts it, 'creeping suburbia, deadlier than any weed, has blighted the pastoral loveliness of the walk'. Shottery is just a mildly inconvenient outpost of Stratford now, and particularly best avoided at summer weekends.

Then, go in winter. Best of all, walk there in frost and deep, deep snow, down the low-lying lane to the famous cottage. It is transformed, the orchard silent, the boughs bare and all the latches cold. There is holly, red as any blood, and a brave breasted robin, great icicles hang down from the thatch like transparent daggers.

Go inside. You can imagine how it would have been, snug, very dark, close-smelling, candle and fire-lit, with strange shadows. It's still how a lot of country people do live, closed in upon themselves and sheltered within thick walls, against cruel winter.

*Anne Hathaway's cottage*

*Crown Imperials in the garden at Anne Hathaway's Cottage*

Anne Hathaway's cottage is a visual cliché on too many tea-trays, chocolate boxes and jigsaw puzzles, popular for generations. Which is a pity, for its romantic associations and very real charms undoubtedly enhance the plain fact that it is an excellent example of a substantial sixteenth-century English country farmhouse. But perhaps a coyly lyrical description from a Victorian writer best conveys the effect it has always had upon the impressionable visitor:

'In its exterior, the cottage is far more akin to what must have been its aspect in the sixteenth century than the Birthplace, while the chief interior room and its latticed windows and great open fireplace and massive beamed ceiling, seem to exhale the very atmosphere of those far-off days when William Shakespeare came a-courting. The whole question of his marriage has, it is true, been cumbered with much dry-as-dust discussion about the prenuptial bond and other matters, but these details may be left in the hands of the antiquaries and lawyers. The ordinary pilgrim visits Shottery in a romantic mood; he can picture a lovely Warwickshire maiden issuing from that ancient doorway to meet the handsome young son of John Shakespeare of Stratford, and with that he is content. Than this picturesque cottage, with its ancient roof-tree and tangled garden of the flowers of old rural England, there could not be a more seemly terminus for a poetic pilgrimage.'

In the stage-struck days of my youth then, it was for the Royal Shakespeare Theatre – then called the Shakespeare Memorial Theatre – that I came to Stratford and I rarely strayed far from its precincts.

Looked at from any angle at all – from the opposite bank of the river, or from Waterside (the road that runs at the back of it), up river from Clopton bridge or down river from the theatre gardens – it is an eyesore, an architectural monstrosity in red brick – though the addition of the new Swan Theatre in 1986 has certainly improved things.

No one could actually say the main theatre is a visual asset, and even allowing for the generally philistine attitude of the local planning authority, I doubt if permission would be granted now for it to be slapped down just there, four-square and uncompromising. Yet I am enormously fond of it, because of past pleasures, and it has all the charm of personal association and long familiarity to very many people. One is used to it, the eye ceases to be offended by the ugliness and simply accepts. Stratford without it is unimaginable.

In any case, it was never what the Royal Shakespeare Theatre looked like that interested or excited me, but what happened there and the general atmosphere surrounding it, what it stood for. And the smell!

The sense of smell is the most potent and affecting of all; it, more than anything else, has the power to attach itself to a time, a place, forever, so that the slightest whiff catapults one straight back into the past. I don't know what the foyer of the Royal Shakespeare Theatre smells *of* – an amalgam of all kind of particular ingredients – but I have only to push open the heavy glass doors and step inside that cool, rather imposing and formal area, and sniff, and I am sixteen again, the queue in which I have been standing for over an hour has at last got within sight of the box office.

There was tremendous camaraderie among those

(Previous page) *The Royal Shakespeare Theatres.* (Left) *The view from the rear of the stage of the Swan Theatre.*

queueing for standing tickets or returns – I imagine there still is; you meet and make firm friends with people standing next to you, from Ohio or Tokyo, Stockholm or Tipperary, swop anecdotes about plays seen, pin-ups among this year's actors, and then part, abruptly, never to see one another again.

The excitement of being front of house was considerable, but for a few years at that time an old friend of my mother's family was in the company, and so I had a passport to the magic world of Backstage. I went round there on summer afternoons, at the end of performances of Redgrave's *Hamlet*, or Dorothy Tutin's *Twelfth Night* – legendary productions, now –

along corridors full of costumes hanging on rails, you could *touch* them as you went by! You might *see* a dressing-gowned Star, on his way to the shower; and the star dressing rooms must be among the nicest in the theatrical world, with French windows opening out onto little balconies that overlook the river; cool air blows in off the water on stuffy nights, there are the shouts of people in rowing boats, happy-holiday noises.

The interior of the main house used to be my favourite sort of theatre, with a curtain and a proper proscenium arch, within which the play was contained:

*The stage of the Swan Theatre and* (right) *Clopton Bridge*

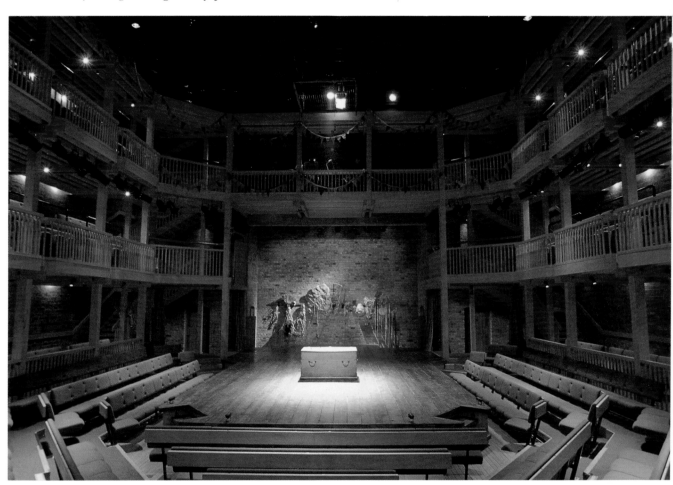

it was another world, apart and separate, lit from within, enticing and yet impenetrable.

Gradually, they have been changing it, doing away with the curtain, extending the stage, rounding off the boxes, trying within the structural limitations of the building to make it both more Elizabethan and more modern, for the fashion now is all against the Victorian, proscenium arch. I hate the fashion. I do not like to be in the middle of the play, to be able to see the sweat and the spittle, to have a back and a side as well as a front view of the actors, it makes me feel embarrassed and uneasy, destroys the precious illusion.

The whole theatre complex has been immeasurably enhanced by The Swan, built onto one end of the main house, beside the garden, with a soaring Gothic roof that makes your heart leap, twin weather vanes like graceful birds, and an exterior of brick that marries so perfectly with the existing buildings that, from the first day it was completed, it looked as if it had been there always, elegant, symmetrical, right.

Inside, it is small, a cockpit of a theatre, and pretty, with lots of wooden boxes ranged in an arc around a projecting stage. It looks Elizabethan, it feels comfortably modern, a triumph of planning and design – and of philanthropy, too, for The Swan was the gift of an anonymous benefactor.

An air of excitement, of anticipation and partici-pation, those are what the theatre generates. You feel it in the air all around the place, among the queuers and the audience spilling out and milling about on the terraces in the interval, and streaming home at the end, talking, laughing, still a bit dazed, as though they are more than half left behind in that other-world, but coming to, flushed with pleasure, in this one. That, more than anything, is what surrounds the whole building, you can feel it, just walking by. If there is ever a sense of Shakespeare being a man dead and lost in history, remembered only in museums and archives and old buildings, then the life of the theatre which exists to present his plays dispels all of that, brings the man and his work into the world as it is now, a new creation every season. Shakespeare lives!

Quite early on Sunday mornings in summer, when-ever I am in Stratford, I go for a walk, down through the empty streets of the little town, across the Bancroft gardens – packed like Brighton beach on Saturday afternoons, deserted now – to the old tramway bridge. On the other side, I follow the tow-path beside the river, up towards the church.

From here, it looks wonderful. It is one of the handsomest buildings I have ever seen, like a great ship in full sail, rising up out of the surrounding trees, its reflection beautiful in the water. It is as handsome as many a cathedral, and less intimidating, perfectly proportioned in a perfect setting. Visitors would surely come from far countries to see it, and for itself alone, never mind that William Shakespeare is buried here.

From where I stand, I wonder how anything could ever spoil this sight of it.

Ah, since 1985 something has, though the hideous-ness is well screened in summer by all that lush and leafy green so the eye is deceived. Then the trees cover the shame. But come here in bare winter and be

appalled at what has been allowed. Your eyes will be hurt enough then.

On summer mornings, I wish I had a ferryman to row me over the water, or a little silent boat tied up, waiting. It's a long way round again, but worth the walk, to come up to the church from the top of Waterside, so that I enter by the avenue of limes that lead a long straight way up to the porch. They are wonderful trees, so tall and graceful, joining hands at the top all the way in a triumphal arch. No bride and groom ever need a guard of honour here, they have a natural one already.

Stand, looking up the avenue, and you cannot help but think of weddings. What bride would not feel ten feet tall and grand as a princess, walking up this path? And especially when the trees rustle slightly, so that the leaves make rippling shadow patterns on the flat stone slabs.

It all looks perfectly symmetrical, in a design that always seems to me romantic but is, in fact, Biblical; there are twelve trees on the left of the avenue to represent the twelve tribes of Israel, but only eleven in line on the right. For there were twelve apostles until Judas Iscariot turned traitor, and so there is a gap, but not completely. Standing back slightly is another tree, for St Mathias, who took Judas's place.

It doesn't matter if you don't know this, the avenue will still take your breath away, but when you do, you feel an extra, poetic sense of rightness.

I like to walk slowly up the avenue but then, just at the church porch, turn right, and take the path that girdles the church and comes out onto the terrace above the river. Here there are comfortable green benches on which to sit and watch the river go by, and the Sunday morning rowers who skim past, swift as blades, and the comfortable, patient fishermen strung out all along the bank.

It's the most pleasing of churchyards because, although well tended, it's never too tidy. The grass is mown, but not like a bowling green all shaven and shorn; there is a bit of a higgledy piggledy of grave-

*Holy Trinity Church, from the river*

stones, some leaning forwards just a little, others swaying back, others sunken down, or beginning to crumble. No one, thank God, has decided to make a clean sweep and line them all up against the perimeter walls, like prisoners waiting to be shot, so that the gardeners can have a clear run with the mowers.

There are a lot of gravestones, and a lot of trees, too, and the trees are interwoven with the graves and complement them because they are all shapes and sizes and nicely irregular, great yews and Scots pines, clipped trees, fat-bellied trees, tall, short, bushy, spindly, leafy, needly, dark, pale, all set about at random. Yet the whole effect, grass and graves and trees, is all of a piece, blending in exactly the right balance.

There are not many new graves, and so no little rose bushes, or pots and vases and urns of various flowers. Indeed, hardly any flowers at all, but perhaps one day someone thought the place lacked brightness, and wanted perking up, so they cut a nice big circular bed, worthy of any municipal park, and stuffed it full of the gaudiest petunias, white and regal purple and vivid red, and there it sits, and you can't pretend it doesn't.

And if you're lucky, early on these summer mornings, you will be the only person wandering about, but you

GOOD FREND FOR IESVS SAKE FORBEARE
TO DIGG THE DVST ENCLOASED HEARE;
BLESE BE Y MAN Y SPARES THES STONES
AND CVRST BE HE Y MOVES MY BONES

(Opposite) *The chancel of Holy Trinity Church on Shakespeare's birthday – 'a floral carpet', and* (above) *Shakespeare's gravestone*

will not be alone. A pair of mallard duck, up from the river, waddle precariously along the wall; a blackbird runs suddenly, silently, low to the ground; a fledgling robin, fluffy, newly launched into the world, sits beside the path, too tame for his own safety. And a foot from your foot, at the base of a tree, a grey squirrel nibbles a nut, turning it around and around between his paws in that most squirrel-ish of postures.

Inside, the Collegiate church of the Holy and un-divided Trinity is majestic, like its name, imposing, and yet not too grand, spacious and lofty, but never echoing and cold. And you never forget that this is a living, working church, a parish church, with a regular and active local congregation, with youth clubs and Sunday School, bell-ringers and bazaars, bible fellow-ship and baptisms, as well as the graves of all the Shakespeares, and the monuments and memorials to great benefactors, and all those visitors from most corners of the earth.

This time, early on Sunday morning, is the time to appreciate it as a real, and somehow, an ordinary church, if you stay to the first Communion Service, and afterwards, sit on, looking up, and all around, admiring, being awed, and at the same time, completely at home, comfortable. The nave is like a barn, broad, foursquare-feeling, with a roof, part ancient, part not, like a wooden patchwork quilt.

It is this mixture of the great and stately and historic, the ancient and the living present that I like so much. And I particularly like the kneelers, always arranged symmetrically in their rightful rows below the chairs, with wool tapestry designs of verses from the Psalms in praise of the Creator, and examples of what one should praise Him for – Showers and Dew, Summer and Winter, Sun and Moon, Stars, Angels, Powers, Heavens.

The stained glass lets the place down, as it so often does the otherwise glorious English Parish Church – though in the north-west corner of the nave there is a good window in honour of the poets, Caedmon, Chaucer and Milton, to keep company with Shakespeare. It's not the design, but the idea that is so pleasing.

Thousands of visitors come into this church every year. They come on foot, bent double under great rucksacks. They come in coaches carrying cameras, in cars carrying maps. I often wonder what strikes them as they wander around, what they are thinking when they walk through the nave towards the chancel and up to the High Altar – to the reason for their visit. How much they really *see*. Whether they can take in very much of the atmosphere, the totality of this church. Perhaps it is so impressive that it somehow stops them in their tracks, and stills them, so that they will ever afterwards remember.

But too few can have the chance of approaching the chancel, and the poet's grave, in the best way of all because they do not have the time or inclination, or are simply there on the wrong day of the week. For the best way is on a Sunday, and in the context of the Communion Service. You have had time to get used to the main body of the building, to relax, think, pray, breathe quietly, *feel* this church. Then, you stand, and take your place in the file, moving up slowly, into the chancel, between the choir stalls of dark carved and polished wood, to kneel at the rails before the High Altar. The early morning sunlight coming through the stained glass windows high above casts lozenges of translucent colour, blood red, purple, gold, onto the grey stone floor. The clergy move to and fro, giving the wafer and the wine. Then, look, and you see them. A line of stone slabs, set in the floor. Resting on them, small, plainly lettered plaques, with the names of those buried here – Thomas Nash, John Hall, Susanna, Anne. Around one, a plain outline of red rope, laid on the ground, not upright to fence it off, merely to emphasise.

Here lies William Shakespeare.
Good Frend for Jesus Sake Forbeare
To Digg the Dust Encloased Heare.
Bleste Be The Man That Spares Thes Stones
And Curst Be He That Moves My Bones.

No one ever has.

In a niche of the wall above the gravestone, the monument to the poet. He looks a little blank and a little pompous, too. This is Shakespeare the man of property and respected burgher of Stratford, not, in spite of the scroll and quill pen, Shakespeare the playwright, poet, man of the theatre, genius.

Quietly to come here, kneel to receive the Communion, quietly to go, and in the course of this, to be for a few moments beside that plain grave, is to somehow set Shakespeare, his life and his work, in the right context.

In this town he lived, to this church he was carried to be christened, here he came to worship, to this church he was brought, through the screen that now stands across the north transept, to be buried. The greatest writer the world has ever known.

Give thanks then, and go, through the low arched doorway which frames a picture of the porch and the lime avenue, out into the sunshine, and the wide world beyond the gate.

★　　★　　★

*The Stratford weir*

But the immediate world beyond the parish church contains more than its fair share of architectural monstrosities. Quite why an area originally so pretty, a setting entirely in keeping, should have been allowed to suffer in this way will never cease to distress, though perhaps not really surprise me, for we seem to have no eye and little care, no sense of rightness and harmony, nowadays. Either bad taste, money or expedience dominate – and, too often, all three.

The parish hall itself, immediately opposite the main entrance to Holy Trinity Church, is not exactly a thing of beauty, though it is not actually ugly either, merely dull and utilitarian and pedestrian. A pity, but the Methodist Church which stands to the left of it, and opposite the side path to Holy Trinity, is another matter, a crude, brash sort of 1960s bungaloid building, and in front of it, reaching to heaven, a spire of quite spectacular ugliness, separate from and adding nothing to the church itself, stuck in the forecourt like a great leaden tripod, as though it would not be outdone by the Anglican spire across the street. Hidden behind some poplars nearby is a charming row of nineteenth-century brick cottages, a backwater of modest domestic architecture of the best kind.

But in front of that, another carbuncle, a 1960s villa at the end of a great sweep of drive and bald lawn, as exposed and bare to the four winds as when it was first built, and all set about with astonishing kitsch – a Temple of Flora, stone lions, flags on ornate flagpoles and assorted statuary.

If it were not where it is, so that it makes one weep, it would perhaps make one laugh. But the development on the site of the house called Avonside, right next to the parish church, is no laughing matter. That is what has been allowed to spoil the perfect view of Holy Trinity, from the opposite side of the river, and what has destroyed the character of once-peaceful Mill Lane.

On the modern principle of cramming as many houses as possible into a given space, flats and maisonettes now stand where, once, gardens alone sloped down to the water. They are uncompromisingly ugly and out of keeping, they crowd in too close to the church, they have ruined the sight of it and the area around it.

Looked at from any angle at all, they make one weep.

A local planning officer was heard to confess ruefully that, with hindsight, they ought never to have been allowed.

Oh, but they were, they were.

★ ★ ★

Holy Trinity Church is the one for a wedding, if that wedding is a grand affair, and many's the one I've ogled at as a passer-by and stander-at-the-gate, with my daughter in her pram waving at the bride and laughing with delight at the confetti.

But the place that is closest to my own heart for a wedding is a few hundred yards away, the small and ancient Guild Chapel, set beside the Grammar School, for it was here, at five in the afternoon on Shakespeare's birthday, 23 April 1975, that I myself was married, on a perfect day of warm spring sunshine and a few high,

*The Avonside development of repellent and incongruous new houses, crammed close to Holy Trinity Church – a breath-taking example of planner's blight. (Opposite) The Guild Chapel, King Edward VI Grammar School and the timbered almshouses*

white clouds, when all the gardens of the town were beautiful with magnolia blossom – one of the prides of Stratford.

There were only a very few of us – five close friends, the vicar, ourselves, and the Sergeant of the Grammar School to make all spick and span for us, and we had our share of minor mishaps. The Archbishop of Canterbury's special licence – the Guild Chapel itself is not licensed for weddings – only arrived that morning, at the wrong address, twenty miles away; the groom had to drive there at speed to fetch it back. And first the Vicar's best pen and then the new husband's best pen ran out of ink, at the signing of the register. Bad omens? Oh, not at all, not at all. It was the happiest of

*The courtyard in front of the King Edward VI Grammar School and* (opposite) *the interior of the school.*

days, we drank champagne in the courtyard that lies between Big School, where Shakespeare was educated, and the Chapel, and the sun shone and shone.

Understandable, then, that I should have such an affection for the Guild Chapel, but I would love it in any case, it is so cool, so quiet, so light, so plain. It feels romantic, with the bare, bleached wooden pews all facing inward to the aisle, the pale stone, the clear glass windows. Nothing superfluous, little decoration, except for the carving on the pews, the rather austere, gilded organ pipes above the stone font.

In the early fifteenth century, there were wall paintings depicting the legend of the Holy Cross, from which the Guild took its name, but they were whitewashed over, and only those over the chancel arch have been partially uncovered, in faded pinks and flesh tints, flaking, blending back into the wall itself.

There are very rarely many visitors here, and they do not linger long, for there is not, perhaps, a great deal to see, but the ancient calm and peace of the place seeps into you if you sit for a time. It is an immensely soothing place.

I have been to concerts in the Guild Chapel – the acoustics are very sweet for solo voices, solo flutes. I

have been at Christmas, the pews packed with locals listening to carols sung by the boys of the Grammar School, and candlelight and lamplight making shadows on the whitewashed walls. I have been to a funeral, too, that of J. B. Priestley, a serious, sad, but not a gloomy occasion, a small gathering of family and friends, saying goodbye to one of England's good men of letters.

And whenever I have been, I have felt all over again how modestly beautiful a chapel it is, standing foursquare at the corner of one of the most ancient and pleasing bits of the town, with the site of Shakespeare's home, New Place, opposite, and the Grammar School and timbered row of almshouses alongside. It makes me glad every time I go by.

Stratford is a busy little town. Busy, in the usual traffic and going-to-work and shopping and domestic sense, and busy with tourists, too; but busy – or perhaps the word is, lively – in other ways, for wherever you stroll, in whatever direction, at any time of the year, there is something going on.

It's partly because of the river, of course; any English town with such a meeting place and focal point as a river, or the sea front, will be humming with activity; also, because of the visitors, for whom entertainment must be provided, but more than all that – the people of Stratford just seem to do such a lot of things, to be joiners-in, putters-on, organisers, performers, participants, to have fun.

One warm evening early one July, we strolled around the centre of the town, the baby daughter in her pushchair, the elder daughter cavorting about. It was the beginning of the Stratford festival, which is fast becoming an annual event, a celebration of music of many kinds, street theatre, children's puppetry, folk dancing, fireworks and all manner of other delights. And the general tourist merrymaking and summer holiday-go-round were in full swing. And I remembered how an American friend, returning to live in Washington after some years here, said that what he would miss most were 'things happening outside in the evenings' – people about the streets, for none of that innocent pleasure can safely go on there.

As we walked slowly through and round the town, I realised exactly what he meant, saw what he would be missing.

There were three plays being performed, one in each of the Royal Shakespeare Theatres, and another, an all boys' performance of *As You Like It*, in the grounds of the Grammar School. In Hall's Croft garden, madrigal singers; in the Shakespeare Institute, a poetry reading; variously scattered about the Bancroft, morris dancers, a ceilidh, a silver band; the Tennis Club was holding a barbecue, the Art Society was displaying pictures, and men walked about on stilts handing out festival leaflets.

And every pub and bar and café and restaurant was full, and as usual on summer nights, the customers overflowed the Dirty Duck on Waterside, and lay all about the grass of the theatre garden, drinking beer beside the nine men's morris. The atmosphere was alive yet relaxed, a muddle of music and laughter and motor car horns, innocent, happy.

On any summer Sunday, go down to the river and see how much goes on. The early rowers, in singles and pairs and eights, seriously sculling, the canoeists; the narrow boats are lined up against the bank, and people emerge sleepily, to stretch in the early air and breathe in the river smells, and take their mugs of tea to drink up on the roof. Later, there will be couples and happy families rowing about, and the long boats, the *Titania* and the *Maid Marian*, plying up and down, full of passengers, enjoying the view of the town from the water.

In winter, superficially, Stratford is all different – no pleasure boats, no lingering and lolling on the grass, and 'the nine men's morris is filled up with mud'. But in every church hall and public meeting

*The interior of the Grammar School*

place all about the town, there will be aerobic and keep fit and Karate classes, children doing ballet and tap, meetings of pigeon fanciers and local history societies, the retired being lectured to, and evening class students learning foreign languages, and at the parish church, on every Tuesday evening, winter and summer, the bell-ringers meet to practise and fill the streets of Old Town full of their pealing.

And then there are the big, set events, beginning, on the Saturday nearest to 23 April, with the celebrations in honour of Shakespeare's birthday, when the world comes to the town of Stratford and meets with the mayor and corporation, and unfurls flags and carries flowers in procession, from the theatre gardens up through the streets to Shakespeare's Birthplace, and from the Birthplace along to the church. There, the wreaths and the sheaves, the bouquets and the posies are laid like a floral carpet in the chancel beside the grave.

The great British love of pomp and procession is here translated into something both formal, international and touchingly homely. There are ambassadors and diplomatic representatives and all manner of civic dignitaries, mingling with the Grammar School boys in their boaters and the actors and the people of Stratford, and everyone dressed up, gold chains and medals, morning suits, top hats and flowery hats, and all in honour not of a god or a saint or a king – but of a playwright and poet, and a local man made good.

And babies bowl along in prams and pushchairs, and toddlers ride high upon shoulders, and the fun of it all is in the flags fluttering from white poles set like guardsmen all about the town, and the flowers, and the marching and the band. A good day.

In the autumn, a good day of a different kind, for locals and showmen, and children most of all. The

*The Beadle of Stratford leading the Birthday Procession of civic dignitaries and international visitors out of the Birthplace.*

(Opposite) *The Birthday Celebration procession in Bridge Street.* (Above) *The Mop Fair*

annual Mop Fair, when stalls and the fun fair, the roundabouts and the flying wheels, and the dodgems, and all the noisy, smelly diesel engines that drive them, pack the town centre.

By day, it's for small children, but by night for the older and bolder ones, with the nerve to fly sky-high on the terrible machines. You can see the lights for miles, hear the music and the shrieks of delight, and the great Victorian merry-go-round that always stands at the end of Rother Market is a sight to behold, all prancing horses and flying hair, as fast as a top, spinning in the Stratford night.

And the next morning, they are gone, like the Arabs they have folded their tents and slipped quietly away to the next town; it is eerie, going out to where it all so brightly, busily, noisily was, and finding only empty streets.

# Charlecote

There is a nice, very well known story about Shakespeare and Charlecote and it goes back a long way. It was said that as a young man, the poet came here from Stratford to poach the deer in the park, and was caught. Subsequently, he appeared before the magistrate, who happened to be Sir Thomas Lucy, owner of Charlecote and that after Sir Thomas punished him, probably by fining, Shakespeare wrote a ribald rhyme about the magistrate which got him into such hot water that he fled the district – to London, fame and fortune.

There's no evidence at all for any of it, except gossip handed down. My own gut feeling is that, on the no-smoke-without-fire principle, the hard core of the story probably *is* true, but has been improved upon and elaborated down the centuries.

Anyway, it helps to make Shakespeare real, gives genius a human face, and I always think of it when I go to Charlecote. When I lived in Leamington Spa, a few miles away, I used to visit it a lot, driving past it on the back-roads way to Stratford. Nice. Late one fine and frosty night in deepest winter, I had a puncture, just outside the main public gate near the front park and as I knelt, quite alone, in the road to change the wheel, I heard a faint rustling, bumping sound and, looking up, saw a line of deer close up to the fence, their eyes red-rimmed in the light from my headlamps, staring, staring, their breath smoking up in plumes on the cold air. They were strangely comforting, beautiful, blonde-coated creatures with their soft muzzles and wonderful, ridiculous antlers.

Indeed, I remember it best, and love it best, in winter. I have often come and fed the deer on bags of little, hard, windfall apples which they love, and then walked all alongside the paling – the house and grounds are closed, out of season – looking across the park, at the bare trees, the grass white with frost, the deer dotted about, or suddenly taking to their slender heels and galloping gracefully away out of sight.

(Left) *The River Dene flows through the deer park*

There used to be more and finer trees; you could look up not only the grand avenue of limes leading from West Lodge, but through those of the great and late-lamented elms, lost, like all those thousands of others in the English countryside, in the great plague of the 1970s.

The pleasure of Charlecote for me lies all outside. It is a lovely park, not too big, not too grand, manageable rather than over-aweing. This is a slightly dull bit of Warwickshire, rather flat, rather ordinary, but walk up the lime drive, to the gatehouse, and turn right, up the steps and across the lawn towards the orangery. There is a very pretty view of a very pretty tower, that of the church at Hampton Lucy, half a mile away.

Walk to the back of the house, and stand at the top of the steps, and look down at a backwater-bit of the River Avon, quietly moving here, narrow, fringed with reeds and rushes.

Look across West Park, towards the deer barrier, over the river and see a piece of English landscape gardening at its modest best. The gardens are not very big, not very ornate or elaborate, easy to stroll around in a quiet half-hour, and there is a Shakespeare herbaceous border, where everything that should not really go together somehow does, and it makes a happy game, reading out the labels to a companion and making him put the plants to the plays.

You can have tea sitting outside the little Victorian orangery, where a peacock or two will strut and squawk and perhaps display, though someone has painted the nice wrought iron chairs and tables green when anyone with half an eye can see that they ought to be white.

Staying outside the main house, there is a courtyard with a wonderful old herring-bone brick wall leading to stables, and upstairs-downstairs sort of kitchens and scrubbed and tidy sculleries, and all is very harmonious.

Then there is the inside. A good many people go round dutifully, consulting guide books, listening,

*The Elizabethan exterior of Charlecote*

looking respectfully and I daresay they all admire it, and like it better than me, for this is exactly the kind of stately English home interior that many people love but I myself dislike. It is so dark, so stuffed and stuffy, so sombre and over-furnished with such a lot of things I find hideous. There are all those ornate gilded mirrors and picture frames and pompous portraits, the moulded ceilings and heavy draperies, screens and stools and ugly tables.

I am depressed beyond bearing, coming from all that light and air and space and natural gracefulness of the park, into these ornate rooms.

But I like to stand in the great hall and look up, to the picture of the handsome Sir Thomas Lucy III with his family, all posed and poised, little old-looking children with grave faces, clustered around a serene-faced mother. And at a little remove, another, depicting 'Additional children of Sir Thomas Lucy', four even graver, even older-looking little people – and quite nameless.

The whole of Charlecote is heavily restored – put back, as it were, to what it might have been in Elizabethan times. The effect is good, of quite a small, nicely-proportioned English gentleman's seat. But the moment you know that the gatehouse is the one completely unaltered feature, you *see* that it is a perfect, satisfying piece of sixteenth-century domestic architecture in soft rose-coloured brick. It rings the right note.

(Below) *The Great Hall, and* (right) *the sixteenth-century gatehouse.* (Overleaf) *Sunset at Charlecote*

Chipping Campden

Chipping Campden stands exactly on the imaginary border between what you might call the Vale of Shakespeare, and the Cotswolds. It is only twelve miles from Stratford, and as soon as you leave it by that road, you feel instinctively that you are *in* Shakespeare country; yet in architecture, and most of all in spirit, Chipping Campden belongs absolutely to the Cotswolds. It is their most northerly outpost. Although the little town lies in a fold between high ground, sheltered and mellow, it has about it the feel of those bare, windswept, sheep-dotted hills. In summer, it also has rather too much of the feel of an overcrowded tourist spot now, especially at the week-ends. I prefer it at quite other times.

But to appreciate Chipping Campden, you must first come upon it. The approaches are very important. You travel there from Stratford mostly 'on the flat', and although that's the best way to get a first sight of the beautiful curve of the High Street, you don't get any sense of the place in the context of its setting – the jewel in the ring. My favourite way is from the south, travelling via Moreton-in-Marsh and then Blockley. Beyond there, the road is high, and one of the loveliest stretches of English countryside lies below and all around you – modest, unshowy, typical of these leafy inland farming counties.

A lot of people go walking around here. There are well-marked paths to follow, and to toil up these hills with a pack on your back, and then sit on a stone at the top of the highest point and rest, look around, drink it in – that must be the best way of all, except, I suppose, to see it from the back of a horse.

Otherwise, stop the car, get out and, first of all, listen. Even in high summer, on the stillest-seeming day, there is the keening of the wind up here, and in autumn and winter, it cuts across like a steel, beats you about the head. Cotswold winds are cold.

Lately the hedgerows and verges have been left to

*Looking south-east from Chipping Campden.* (Previous page) *Looking east towards the little market town*

grow, the wild flowers are back and, with them, the butterflies and bees. You can hear the grass in all the surrounding fields humming with them. Otherwise, there are sheep bleating, and surprisingly few cars on this minor road, even in the season.

You feel near to the sky here, a sky which always seems to have fast-moving clouds, so that on a windy day the earth feels as if it is spinning, and you with it; it's a heady sensation. When you've had enough of it, look down, across all these broad acres, and there is Chipping Campden, the stone houses and slatey roofs varying in shade according to the play of light, golden and honeyed or harsher, flintier, greyer. It has always seemed to me a haven beckoning to the tired traveller, a place of safety – and so it must have seemed for hundreds of years, to riders, shepherds, coach-passengers. From here, you can see the glory of the church, with its mighty tower topped by four gilded weather vanes like flying angels, which sometimes catch the evening sun and shine so brightly they do indeed seem to be things not of earth but of heaven. After this, it is good to slip rather slowly and quietly down the hill towards the flat road that runs through the thatched, gentrified little village of Broad Campden, between houses, into the town itself.

I've said that my first sight of it was in early spring and it is on those fresh, daffodil-yellow days that it still comes most readily to mind. But the next time I went, the world was in a very different mood, and Chipping Campden revealed itself as a more mysterious place.

It was at the very end of October and, feeling rather beleaguered, I decided to have a weekend away by myself. I was living in Leamington Spa at the time, but I didn't want to travel too far. I couldn't have chosen better than Chipping Campden; it looked and felt like another world, somehow cut off, in its own strange, self-contained atmosphere. I felt that I was going back in time as well as away in distance.

*View towards Broadway, and* (overleaf) *the church of St James*

I arrived as it was getting dark, though it was only tea-time, and the sky was thick with great pot-bellied rain clouds. Because I'd had someone to visit first, I came in on the road from Cheltenham and Broadway, near Dover's Hill and, since I was there, I got out of the car and walked over the thick clumpy grass to look over what always seems like a precarious shelf on the edge of the world. But the sky was gathering, the land was dark, there was a cold mist and low cloud like cobwebs in my face. On a clear day, you can see from Dover's Hill across to the Vale of Evesham and the blue line of the Malvern Hills beyond, and over the valley of the Avon too. It is a wonderful place for children – to roll over and over down the tussocky slopes, to fly kites, to run and run and run. But on this lowering afternoon, I was alone there, it was bleak, dismal, and a little sinister, too. I kept glancing over my shoulder as I hurried back to my car.

By the time I reached the High Street, it was pouring with rain; never have lighted rooms, and glimpses of flickering fires within, looked more inviting. Yet after unpacking and a cup of tea in my hotel, I went out again – because of something or other in the air, the smell of the autumn rain damping down bonfires. There is always something attractively melancholy and romantic about such a night.

One of the charms of Chipping Campden is the line of small shop windows which intermingle with ordinary domestic front rooms along the High Street, with the butcher, the baker and the candlestick-maker next to the souvenir pottery and pretty gifts, all in those ancient stone houses. They've taken care not to make a mess of the shop fronts here – no garish hoardings and boardings, everything is tasteful, at least to outward show. And because this is very much a town where real people live, not just a tourist stop, Campden still

(Opposite) *St James from the churchyard, and* (right) *the Woolstaplers Hall*

has plenty of real shops for them, supplying ordinary domestic needs. It is one of the reasons I like it so much, and prefer it to Broadway, that coach-stop full of antiques and tea-rooms which always looks as if it is packed flat into cardboard boxes and put away at the end of the summer season.

But on a windy wet autumn night, Chipping Campden is very much all there, yet deserted. As the shops closed and their lights went out, and people drew curtains tight against the black outside, the streets of Chipping Campden became silent, except for my footsteps.

I walked up the slope, past the almshouses, a row of buildings utterly fitting to their honourable purpose and, as I neared the church gate, I began to feel that on such a night, rather than in the traditional moonlight, the ghosts of Campden might walk. At the bottom of the avenue that slopes up to the church porch, I stopped, hearing the pattering of rain on stone, the rustling of the late leaves on those dark, dark trees.

And walked quickly back, to the chintzy comfort and log-fire safety of the hotel.

The next morning, the town was rinsed clear and clean of rain, there was a wind whipping down the High Street, busy with the ladies of Campden and their shopping baskets, and the sky was a bright, hard blue. I went up to the church then happily enough. And oh, it is beautiful, so very imposing, a mighty monument to all those men made rich on the backs of the sheep in medieval England. The church is the finest of its kind in the Cotswolds, and all of a piece with the rest of the town, although it so dominates it. It ought to seem simply too big yet oddly, it doesn't.

That's why I can never decide what I like best about the town, whether any particular corner is nicer than the rest, it is so all-of-a-piece. But the curve of the almshouses, the road that slopes up and around to the

church, the light, lofty, airy interior of the church itself and the views over the countryside from the churchyard, these never fail to give me new pleasure every time I visit.

I like the row of eight bells outside the ancient public house of that name (which used to be entirely frequented by gnarled locals with impenetrable Cotswold accents, who looked hard through any stranger, but must be a bit more of a visitors' establishment nowadays, because they have avocado pears on the bar-lunch menu).

I like the museum of curious artefacts in the Woolstaplers Hall – ancient cameras, and early vacuum cleaners alongside lead soldiers and suits of armour. And the gravestone of the furniture designer Gordon Russell, who lived and worked in Campden and is buried in the churchyard – it has an owl on top.

And all the stone alleyways, cool and dark between houses, with bright gardens glimpsed beyond. The window ledges set about with bits of old china, and sweet peas or geraniums crammed into pots.

I love the tea rooms, the snug hotels, the shadows thrown by the arches of the market hall, the little lanes that lead in and out of one another around the back of the High Street. I love the smallness of the shops, the overcrowded interiors, the shape of the windows, the breadth of the main street.

Indeed, everything in Chipping Campden seems harmonious. If you look along the High Street, you will see houses dating from as far back as the fourteenth century, and others very much of the classical eighteenth century, and yet all blend together and balance one another and all continue to form such a perfect whole.

It has got busier: there are some rather ugly new houses faced (at the local planner's insistence) in raw, new Cotswold stone in depressingly even-sized slabs that look incongruous on a 1960s-style semi-detached and have still not mellowed or weathered acceptably. But you can ignore them, drive quickly by, and although there are, inevitably, more cars, more people, Chipping Campden is still, especially out of season, an unspoilt, tucked-away, self-contained sort of place.

(Below and opposite bottom) *Fish Hill outside Chipping Campden;* (opposite top) *a view of Aston Subedge*

# Hidcote Manor Gardens

The garden at Hidcote Manor was created, from 1910 onwards, by Major Lawrence Johnston, an American who spent most of his life in England. Of his accomplishment, Vita Sackville-West wrote an eloquent appreciation:

'When Major Johnston first acquired Hidcote, he had nothing as a basis to his garden except one fine cedar and two groups of beeches. The rest was just fields and I cannot believe that to any but a most imaginative eye it can have seemed a very promising site. There was no particular shape to it; standing high, it was somewhat wind-swept; there was nothing in the nature of old walls or hedges to afford protection; the soil was on the heavy side. It must have required immense energy, optimism, foresight and courage to start transforming it into what it is today – a matured garden full of variety and beauty, the achievement of one man in his lifetime.

'The combination of botanical knowledge and aesthetic taste is by no means axiomatic, but Major Johnston possessed it in the highest degree. To my mind, Hidcote is a flawless example of what a garden of this type should be.'

On that cold, bright October morning, I drove out to Hidcote, and caught the gardens on the day before they closed for the winter. That was twenty years ago. No one else at all was there on that tail-end-of-the-season morning. I doubt if I should be so lucky now. In the National Trust Directory, it warns ominously that Hidcote is 'liable to serious overcrowding on Bank Holiday weekends and on fine Sundays'. Oh, yes indeed, and to scarcely *less* serious overcrowding on most other days in spring and summer and well into the autumn, too. It has become one of the most popular and visited gardens in the country, about as popular as Sissinghurst, and it seems to me that in spite of the beauty of the flowers, there is simply no pleasure left at all in going there at any time between early June and mid-September. In my ideal world, all such places would stay open all the year round.

Besides, I don't think you need to see it at the height of the summer burgeoning to see it at its best. True, there are some magnificent roses, some fine herbaceous borders – but you can see good roses and herbaceous borders anywhere. There is some unusual planting, there are many rarities, but it is the way these contribute to the whole pattern, the 'green architecture' of the place that I think matters. The joy and uniqueness of Hidcote is in its grand overall design and landscaping, its trees, avenues, vistas, in the amazing fact that the whole place was carved, as it were, out of the unpromisingly bare fields on a cold Cotswold hillside by one man, Major Lawrence Johnston, and begun as recently, in Great Garden terms anyway, as 1910.

There always seems more of Hidcote than there

*A cottage in Hidcote Bartrim village*

actually is, so wonderfully planned was it. Even when it is quite crowded, you can still have the illusion of almost losing yourself. But I remember the feeling of privilege and spaciousness as I wandered around it that autumn morning. I think it was the first time I had ever fully appreciated what it meant to design a garden. I walked on the soaking wet grass up the Long Walk between tall, carved hedges of hornbeam, and when I got to the end, I thought I would round a corner and surely come upon ghosts, ladies and gentlemen in eighteenth-century dress, strolling silently about. It is that sort of place, theatrical, illusions are easily created there.

On summer evenings they have occasionally performed *A Midsummer Night's Dream* at Hidcote on the theatre lawn which is surmounted by a great, ancient beech. It's easy to see why, easy to imagine Puck and the fairies slipping in and out between trees, Bottom and Titania lying in the long grass. Outdoor theatre anywhere in the world is one of the most exciting, evocative, romantic of art-forms, and in this setting, given exactly the right weather, can be haunting, unforgettable.

I suppose it was the air of romantic melancholy that so affected me on that morning, with the leaves suddenly swirling down, and the deep, still, silent pond, the sad bleating cries from sheep in the field beyond the ha-ha. I have dreamed about Hidcote, looking like this, many times since but have never seen it so perfect, and deserted, again.

The next day, I drove by all the back roads, single-tracks across country, with marvellous views from the top of steep hills, breathtaking above Ilmington and then down into the autumnal lanes of Warwickshire, and along beside all the little rivers and streams that crisscross the Shakespeare country, and so home to Leamington.

I've never made that particular journey again, fearing to break some spell that lies over the past, but it's all still there, for anyone else to discover.

*Fields near Ilmington.* (Overleaf) *Maltmill Lane, Alcester*

# Around Alcester

*Delightful close of houses in Church Street, Alcester*

If you draw a ring around the immediate Shakespeare counties and divide the resulting circle into segments, you discover, when travelling within them, that each segment seems to be a little different from the others, to have a different character, look, mood.

Of course, this happens in most English counties which are so richly, minutely varied within their individual, man-made boundaries. It is partly the simple result of geographical features – whether there are hills or not, whether the Avon runs through a particular segment, or one of the other small rivers that vein the countryside, whether it is well-wooded, contains one of the larger towns, has predominantly sheep, dairy, or fruit farming, is relatively more affluent, boasts historic houses and castles, and so on.

Having lived in and around these places for so long, and driven in and out of each segment so often, I can see the changes between each one as they first begin, the subtle difference in the rise of the land, the colour of the fields.

If you go out of Stratford to the south west, it isn't long – only once you are over the top of Bordon Hill – before the land begins to look a little different, because this is where the first fruit orchards appear. You are on the Evesham road, going towards that famous Vale of apples and plums, of pears and asparagus, with its wonderfully rich soil and moist, sheltered air.

In spring, you ride along on a foaming tide of blossom, and so do hundreds of other people, too, for the route is a favourite one for coach outings – and, particularly it seems, of elderly people. And on a sunny late April day of warm breeze and little puffy

*The Vale of Evesham in the spring*

white clouds in an azure sky, it is utterly English, utterly charming, straight out of A. E. Housman. However jaded and world-weary you may be, you catch your breath at all that pink and whiteness, in spite of yourself.

From the late spring, too, the roads and lanes are set about with open stalls selling fresh garden produce, in every other farm and cottage gateway there is a board chalked up with notices of that day's availability: asparagus, potatoes, peas and beans, honey, flowers. It sounds like a garden of Eden, a cornucopia of growing things, and so it can be, but there are so often cold springs, when late snow-storms and sudden gales dash the blossom, blacken it, and blight the hopes of all the farmers in a single night. I have searched here for signs of spring on May days as cold as January.

But if spring is so often treacherous, there is some-thing particular about autumn, an indefinable smell in the air, that never fails to delight me, and in this part of the Shakespeare country where Warwickshire blends into Worcestershire, autumn is always beautiful. If you come out early in the morning, there will be a pearly mist, damp and chill, with dew on the grass and exquisite cobwebs strung delicately across the bars of every wooden gate and stretched over hedges like lace laid out to dry.

Turn off the Evesham road right towards Lower Binton, and up the hill through that clutch of villages not many people seem to know, except those who live there – Temple Grafton, Ardens Grafton, Exhall, Wixford. The lanes wind in and out, up and down, at every turn there is a group of pretty cottages, with smart newer houses in between, and flower baskets, tubs, window boxes, climbers, creepers everywhere. By the time you reach the highest point, and stop in any gateway to look across the golden ripe or newly-cut cornfields towards the Evesham Vale, the sun will come piercing through, and you can watch the mist shrink back, dissolve into nothing, that magical trick of nature.

This little triangle of villages between the two main roads, together with some of those that lie below, has a lot of dubious Shakespeare legends clinging to it. I don't believe in them, whereas I do believe in the Charlecote deer-poaching story, but ask me why and I can't tell you.

But the best of them bears repeating, because though it will have lost nothing in the telling over the centuries, it gives a clue either to how the poet *was* or how people liked to *think* that he was – and perhaps that's just as interesting.

Shakespeare is reputed to have joined a group of Stratford topers who had a drinking contest against those of Bidford, and had been found sleeping off his hangover under a crab-apple tree. When roused by his friends, he is said to have said that he had drunk with

Piping Pebworth. Dancing Marston.
Haunted Hillborough. Hungry Grafton.
Badgering Exhall. Papist Wixford.
Beggarly Broom and Drunken Bidford.

I like the way most of these Shakespeare legends make him out to be both one of the locals, and 'one of the lads', a man given to behaving like any other – it somehow makes his poetry seem even more remarkable.

And once you have the rhyme in your head, it runs obligingly through whenever you pass the sign or see the name of Haunted Hillborough or Piping Pebworth or Beggarly Broom, and stamps a distinctive identity on this quiet corner.

Leave the Graftons, cross the Stratford to Alcester road and, again, the feel of the area changes subtly, for now you are just perceptibly on the way to Birmingham and the Black Country. There are a great many, very heavy lorries passing this way – far too many for what is really just a relatively narrow country road, and to a lot of people, the town of Alcester must simply be a place passed through on the way to somewhere more important.

And that is a pity, because if you turn off the main through-road, into the market square and stop beside the parish church, you will discover one of the most picturesque and pleasing small corners in all the whole Shakespeare country – indeed, perhaps, in England at all. What is important about these few square yards is the rich variety of modestly perfect examples of domestic architecture.

I don't remember a time when I didn't enjoy looking at houses – ordinary, English, lived-in houses of almost every period, streets of small houses, rows of shops, crescents, avenues, lanes, parades of them, as well as individuals. As I grew up, I learned to look, as it were, to some purpose, as well as with enjoyment, taught, like so many people, by John Betjeman, John Piper, Sir Nikolaus Pevsner and latterly, by Alec Clifton-Taylor. And Alcester gives me especial pleasure, it combines so much that is attractive, beautifully proportioned, well preserved but not fossilised. This is a real, living, working town, not a tourist spot, not a museum-place.

The houses, dating from the medieval and half-timbered, through the Elizabethan, to the classically elegant Regency, the handsome Victorian, are set in a curve around the church, and in lanes leading off the market square, and if you look up, all the time, above the level of the front doors, there is something delightful at every turn. Nothing is too symmetrical either, all the houses are set slightly higgledy-piggledy, they do not match, in height or style, or detail, yet they all fit satisfyingly together.

I would far sooner wander about this corner of Alcester than round many a stately home – of which, in fact, there are two within only a mile of the town, Coughton

Court and Ragley Hall. They could scarcely be more unlike each other. Coughton was begun in the sixteenth century, and has very much an Elizabethan air about it, though there are some curious later additions. Ragley is an imposing, very obviously seventeenth-century house. Coughton seems relatively small, it doesn't intimidate, and its rather neat, plain gardens are compact. Ragley stands in extensive parkland, and the whole thing is much grander – it aims to impress.

What they have in common is that both are family houses, and although open to the public on certain days in the summer season, both are still lived in by the present descendants of the original owners. And you can tell, there is, at least to some extent, a slightly domestic air to them, a lightening of that deadness that

*The front and back of Coughton Court*

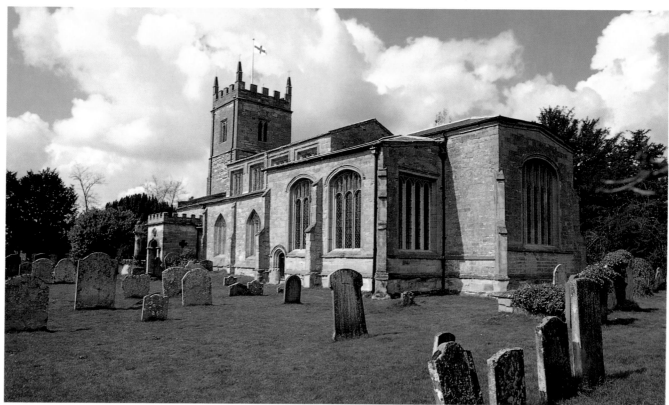

(Opposite top) *View from the gatehouse and* (opposite bottom) *Coughton church.* (Above) *The front of Ragley Hall*

lies like a pall over those historic houses which are now only showpieces and museums.

Coughton, which has an honourable and rather exciting history, is the home of the great English Roman Catholic family, the Throckmortons; as always, I read respectfully about the past of a home but never get very much sense of it when there. There are plenty of the usual, oddly assorted curiosities – including mementoes of the Archdukes of Austria, an ornate cope reputedly embroidered by Catherine of Aragon, the abdication letter of Edward VIII.

Last time I went there, it was quite busy and I roamed restlessly in and out of panelled and tapestried rooms feeling more than usually claustrophobic. Then, out of an upper window, I saw swifts wheeling about in the courtyard, house martins coming in to nest under the beautifully carved wooden eaves – they made the whole place come alive; if there had been a cat on an armchair, it would have been even better. And then, in a dark corner, a glass case containing a very simple, plain cotton gown, embroidered at the neck (in Latin), 'the chemise of the holy martyr, Mary Queen of Scots'. On a small typed notice, it states that in this garment she was beheaded at Fotheringay.

Relics of this kind perhaps always have a ghoulish fascination, but I find this one very moving, perhaps because it *is* tucked away, not drawing attention to itself, but more, because it is very beautiful and in such contrast with all the ornate decoration and furnishings around it.

It seems wrong to say that it gave me pleasure to look at it – but it did, in a sad sort of way. I couldn't get it out of my mind. As we drove away, however, my husband remarked that he thought he'd seen another robe in which she had been beheaded, somewhere quite different. Ah well.

But across the grass beside the house is the (Anglican) church that serves Coughton and four other villages. I always like to go into churches, looking not for the obvious but the unexpected. I found it, in the church-yard first – a great chest tomb with reliefs on the side, depicting a ship and a riderless horse, and a strange Tuscan sundial. Inside, there are Throckmorton tombs, and some lovely brasses, and a seventeenth-century slate memorial slab set into the floor of the nave, with the most touching of verses about the young couple buried below:

> Tho here their beds so closely joyned and set,
> That both are clothéd with one coverlet.

The exterior of Coughton Court has suffered badly

from the loss of the elm avenue which used to frame the view of it from the main road. But the front of the house, the various bits of which don't seem to fit together, is not the best part; it reminds me of a cardboard cut-out of a house, and looks as if it might be *only* a façade, without anything behind it.

The back is quite different and altogether more harmonious. If you walk across the grass and look back, you see it at its best: it forms three sides of a square, with the fourth missing, and the house is gabled and timber-framed, roses climb the walls, lavender beds outline the lawn. Turn your back on the house, and you look across a plain, open field up to a slope on which cattle graze. It makes a very satisfying, uncluttered picture.

The exterior of Ragley takes the breath away, seen from the far side of the deer park. It is a most harmonious-looking, elegant house, everything is somehow *balanced* – the tall windows, the balustraded roof, the porticoes. From whichever side you approach it, it dominates the landscape and its own park, and yet blends with it, and 'every prospect pleases'.

But although the house is stately and sumptuous, it is lived-in, by the present Marquis of Hertford, who has restored it to its former glory, and although the Great Hall makes you gasp, it somehow doesn't make you feel insignificant – nor, surprisingly enough, does it feel chill. Outside in the grounds, there are nature trails, woodland walks, an adventure playground – it's a happy place for children and dogs to picnic, stroll, sit about, explore. It hasn't the fun-fair feel of some of the more commercially-run stately homes, either, and when you go there, the visitors always seem to be English people, families from Stratford or Henley-in-Arden or Redditch enjoying an outing, or Arrow villagers briskly walking their dogs beside the river. Ragley is, as it were, their 'local' stately home.

*The Great Hall at Ragley, and* (overleaf) *Ragley Hall seen from across the park*

Henley-in-Arden and two jewels

Going north out of Stratford, towards Birmingham, you might expect that the road would take you through a trail of ugly suburbs, merging into the outskirts of the Second City, with industrial estates, dirty factories, and universal dullness.

In fact, once you are clear of the rather messy sprawl on this side of Stratford, there is open country-side for much of the route, with undulating fields, and low, wood-crowned hills, and the broad highway runs through trim commuter villages into – well, yes, suburbs, but airy, leafy, well-built and not unattractive ones.

For the first ten miles or so, this is still the Forest of Arden country, and though the trees are no longer matted densely together, there are plenty of them left in between the farmland, though Henley-in-Arden bears little more than the name as a reminder of its original setting.

Henley is a market town suffering the fate of all those ancient English settlements which now have a main arterial road running through the middle of them. It has a long, wide and singularly handsome High Street, lined with an assortment of extremely good-looking smallish, lowish houses, a mixture of black-and-white timbered Elizabethan, white and pink-faced Georgian, with a little of the twentieth-century bow and bay and flat-fronted windows, blending delightfully together.

When you cross the High Street, you take your life in your hands. Heavy lorries, trucks, transporters, private cars, thunder and bang through Henley all day and half the night, making everyday domestic life unpleasant and hazardous to the local people and the noise-level intolerable. Not surprisingly, they were among the most vociferous campaigners for the exten-sion of the M40 link between Oxford and Birmingham and that road is due to be completed in the early 1990s. But in 1986, Henley-in-Arden was distressed to

*The Guildhall, Henley-in-Arden.* (Previous page) *The Forest of Arden in spring*

be told by the traffic planners that the motorway was expected to make very little difference to the volume of vehicles plunging through its heart. Henley will not, after all, become a peaceful backwater once again, or a sleepy market town. What it really needs is a bypass, though, recalling the fate of Warwick to which a bypass made precious little difference, I am sceptical about that proposed solution.

Meanwhile, Henley thrives – a busy, friendly place with a heterogeneous mixture of residents who work locally, in Stratford, in Solihull or in Birmingham, a lot of children, a lot of the elderly, a splendid market-day and, crowning it, to the east, a piece of high ground called the Mount, which is a fine vantage point from which to overlook the roofs and back gardens of the town and, on a clear day, see across a wide area of the countryside.

You reach the Mount by going up Beaudesert Lane, near the market cross, past the ancient and lovely church of Beaudesert, and through a gate. In spring and autumn, you will need wellington boots, in summer, you can take a picnic. But the Mount is best of all on a cold, bright afternoon in winter when the snow is thick on the ground, for then the Mount will be scattered all over with little children, bright as gnomes in red and blue and yellow, pulling toboggans uphill and rushing on toboggans down again, cavorting, snowballing, fighting in heaps. It's a place for families and dogs, a happy place, the air is full of piping voices, and the steep slope is worth climbing; at the top, you feel like the King of the Castle, and if you are young, in years or at heart, you can actually roll all the way down to the bottom again.

A mile or so out of Henley, turn right off the main road, following signs to Lapworth, and you are in the little lanes of leafy Warwickshire again, bumping over canal bridges – though the cottages don't belong to country men but to businessmen, and because this is a

*The Mount seen from Beaudesert churchyard*

prosperous and highly-priced area, everything looks slightly over-trim, the hedges are efficiently, electrically clipped, burglar alarms are prominent.

From here, it is only a few minutes to two of the brightest jewels in the crown owned by the National Trust – Packwood House which has been open to the public since just after the last war, and that most charming, Elizabethan moated manor, Baddesley Clinton, only handed over in 1980. I'd never visited there, but I used to go to Packwood quite often as it made a highly suitable day's outing for visiting elderly relatives.

I often wonder how much it matters to be aware, when visiting one of these old houses, that all is not as it seems – this room or that room has been gutted and re-built in the last fifty years; that wall which seems so ancient, is a replacement, none of it actually started out just so, when first built four hundred years ago. If you are a purist, perhaps it does matter, but I simply like a place, or I don't. It either looks and feels good, all-of-a-piece and pleasing, or it doesn't.

Packwood House has been heavily altered, restored, re-built, converted, but it works, it is delightful, though the exterior, once Elizabethan wood-frame and brick, was rendered in the nineteenth century and rendering always makes a house look dull and depressing, it's too reminiscent of 1920s pebble-dash and 1960s concrete.

Inside, it's a house to thrill a child or a writer of farces, all nooks and crannies, and exits and entrances. It is heavily, darkly wood-panelled which makes it gloomy, particularly in those typically dead-feeling, airless small sitting-rooms, and canopied, tapestried, claustrophobic bedrooms. But the pride of Packwood are the Great Hall and the Long Gallery, which joins it to the house – both constructed between 1925–32 and supremely successful.

The Great Hall was made out of a barn, and was once used as a cow-byre, and it has the original, wooden beams like an inverted rib-cage in the roof.

*The entrance of Packwood House*

(Opposite top) *The Great Hall at Packwood House, and* (opposite bottom) *the Ireton Room.* (Above) *The South or Carolean garden containing the sunken garden*

The Long Gallery is wood-panelled and wood-floored, and has a low ceiling with beams laid along it like a row of ladders, and it would be dark but the light falls in rectangles from the tall windows on the left, one after another, and when the sun comes through, the dust dances in the sunbeams. A good place to pace thoughtfully up and down, up and down. For children, a wonderful place for sliding, skating, ball-rolling – if they were ever allowed to do it.

I often feel sorry for children, trailing disconsolately around Great Houses, but not at Packwood. In the house, there are endless hidey-holes, and in the gardens, there are the trees. Not the normal, common-or-garden beech and ash and oak and larch trees which so beautifully fringe the outlying meadows. No, the strange, surrealistic, slightly frightening yew trees, rows of them, and all clipped closely into the shape of obelisks. They cast long, long shadows. They might be great chessmen, forever standing still in their rows. You can run in and out of them, become lost among them, confused by them. At night, you might imagine all manner of ghosts gliding between them.

At the top of the sloping lawn, there is one huge, round tree, like a sort of cheese-dome, and a path winds around and around actually inside it, so that you reach the top where there is a circular wrought-iron seat. From here you shout to the mystified followers below you, but you cannot be seen. The yew garden is a place of games and dreams and nightmares.

There are other, friendlier delights out here, too. A wonderful long brick wall containing a series of little arched indentations – they are bee-boles for bee skips. A sunken garden with a flat lily pond and a pretty fountain; a gravelly terrace that scrunches under your feet as you walk sedately, or run crazily, between some of the best herbaceous borders I have seen for many a day: little flights of round steps like low tiers on a wedding cake. And lots and lots of good, plain, flat, emerald green grass. And all around it, the parkland, the stately trees, the cows-in-the-water-meadows of rural Warwickshire.

A couple of miles to the east of Packwood lies Baddesley Clinton to which, until 1986, I had never been –

indeed, of which I had never even heard, though in the days before it was given to the National Trust, it was open to the public sometimes when the owner was valiantly struggling to maintain it himself. Now, its future is secure which, I realised the moment I set eyes on it, is a cause for rejoicing for Baddesley Clinton is a gem, a place of pure delight.

We visited it on a mellow, golden afternoon in early September. Blue sky, warm sunshine. Brown bees, the first apples. Grape vines heavy with tiny, dark grapes on the conservatory wall.

At first, you don't see the house at all. You walk from the car park into a grassy courtyard, enclosed on four sides by outbuildings, stables, barns, grain stores, all of which have been impeccably repaired and restored. Here we sat at gingham-clothed wooden tables in the sunshine, and enjoyed that most conventional, traditional, delightful of treats, English afternoon tea, with – as visitors to National Trust properties feel they have a right to expect – home-made scones with strawberry preserve and cream, and chocolate cake. Even if you don't want to eat, go into the refreshment room which has been converted from the barn, because the roof is beautiful.

We lingered for a long time, basking, while the children romped about on the grass, and then we strolled through a gateway and across a short yard, following the signs 'To the house'.

But whenever I visit a place – some historic house, great castle or the tiniest most tucked-away of village churches, I know what I think about it, what delights me or does not, within minutes. But I like to check my quite unprofessional opinion against that of an authority. So, when I returned from that first visit to Baddesley Clinton, I reached at once for the great Nikolaus Pevsner's *Buildings of England*. And glowed with satisfaction, for he says:

'As you approach Baddesley Clinton Hall, it stands before you as the perfect late medieval manor house. The entrance side of grey stone, the small, creeper-clad

*Baddesley Clinton from across the garden*

Queen Anne brick bridge across the moat, the gateway with a porch higher than the roof and embattled – it could not be better.'

I'd not expected anything so good. Baddesley Clinton is not very large. It was built in the fifteenth century, a handsome – no, a *pretty* manor house, entirely surrounded by a moat. Walk all around it, look at the cool reflections in the water, of the house on one side and the fringe of trees on the other, and it reminds you of one of the ancient buildings of Bruges that dip into the still canals.

The only way across the moat into the house is by a short bridge – it may once have been a drawbridge – that leads to a crenellated gatehouse, and so on through a stone passage into a tiny courtyard, bisected by brick paths and bright flowerbeds. It ought, by its design, to be altogether grander, mightier, huger than it is, it's almost a miniature of a fortress, which is also a fairly modest-sized house. The whole design might not have worked, but it does, the proportions are exactly right, utterly satisfying to the eye.

I always like the outsides of houses best. The interior of Baddesley Clinton interested my elder daughter more than it did me. It contains some curiosities, and a lot of oddities. The most astonishing thing in the kitchen is where, beneath a glass viewing panel in the floor, you see a drain – the narrow entrance to which gave access to a hiding place for Catholic priests and monks during the terrible years of the Reformation. In the 1590s, the only way down to it was through a secret hole in the floor of the sacristy above that led into a narrow shaft. Poor, brave, desperate men.

I went back, out into the sunlight, to sit beside the moat and look down at the reflections in the water. Everything seemed peaceful, beautiful, safe. Behind me, the long grass on the edges of the lawns leading away, to fields. To the right, the lovely walled orchard garden, sheltered and secluded.

*The moat on the north side of Baddesley Clinton, and (overleaf) the Great Hall*

'I know a bank whereon the wild thyme blows,
Where oxslips and the nodding violet grows;
Quite over-canopied with luscious woodbine,
With sweet musk-roses and with eglantine.'
(Midsummer Night's Dream)

'The even mead that erst brought sweetly forth
The freckled cowslip, burnet and green clover.'
(Henry V)

'And in the wood, where often you and I
Upon fair primrose beds were wont to lie.'
(Midsummer Night's Dream)

*The wild garden at Baddesley Clinton*

Kenilworth

It takes a certain amount of application nowadays to discover the charms of the small town of Kenilworth. Like so many places of its kind, the twentieth century, and proximity to the industrial and commercial Heart of England, has taken its toll: much that was old and fine – medieval, timber-framed houses on the road to Warwick, for example – has been destroyed. Much is hidden, crowded out, overlaid. Kenilworth, built rather in the shape of a cross, with a long, narrow high street, has become a dormitory town for Coventry, Warwick and Leamington. The tentacles of new housing estates reach out in all directions, spreading over the leafy countryside, traffic is bad, and somehow the whole place has lost much of its character – though I have known many people who live very happily there and it has a vigorous community life.

But you might arrive in it, drive through, wander about, without discovering the best of it. Abbey Fields are sloping, wide open recreation grounds, bordered by some extremely handsome houses, and with wonderful views. On a clear day up there in winter, you can see far across the countryside, towards north Warwickshire, the Malverns, the Cotswolds. It's a happy place, full of children, pram-pushers, dogs, the strolling elderly.

*Snow and drifts at Kenilworth Castle*

*The ruins of Kenilworth Castle*

But whilst other towns have good open spaces, nowhere else in the Shakespeare country is there anything like the mighty pride of Kenilworth – its castle. It is ruined, yes, but enough is left to give you a very clear idea of how it must originally have been, and it gives off an air of history, makes the remote past seem close, more strongly than perhaps anywhere else in the entire area.

It is also a quite wonderfully romantic castle, especially if you visit it late on a winter's afternoon, say, when the blood red sun is setting into banks of dark, dark cloud. You can walk through the ruins and climb up onto the battlements, and imagine almost anything at all – ghosts, the wild cries of invading soldiers in the marshy fields below, or melancholy kings, pacing these same walls, brooding, plotting! It encourages vivid fantasies, and dramatic visions.

The wind whistles and moans in and out of the arrow-slits and around the jagged, broken turrets, and when real sheep send their eerie, abandoned cries across the countryside on the evening air, shivers can run up the spine. Few places I have known have given me such *frissons*. So much is no longer there and yet, in the great hall, with its remarkably preserved and very beautiful windows, there is enough to suggest how it once was, roofed over, furnished, crowded with people. Yet the fact that it is open to the sky, and that grass grows underfoot, and all is stark and bare of ornament, makes it a sad, haunted place – haunted but, to me, quite unfrightening.

Its history is vivid and bloody enough, though. It started life as a medieval castle, ended it as an Elizabethan palace, before being deliberately half blown to bits after the Civil War. So you can imagine it during any historical period you like, from the twelfth century and the reign of King John, through Tudor times to the years of Roundheads and Cavaliers, fill it with soldiers in armour or courtiers in ruffs, imagine professional soldiers keeping the battlements through long night watches over the still, dark fields, or the great banquets and pageant when Elizabeth I arrived for a visit of twelve days in 1575.

> Her Majesty, proceeding toward the inward Court, passed on a bridge, the which was rayled on both sides. And in the toppes of the postes thereof were set sundrie presents, as wine, corne, frutes, fishes, fowls, instruments of musicke and weapons for martial defence. All which were expounded by an Actor, clad like a poet . . . This speech being ended, she was received into the inner Court with sweet musicke. And so alighting from her horse, the drummes, fyfes and trumpets sounded; wherewith she mounted the stayres and went to her lodging.

Needless to say, legend has it that the young Shakespeare must certainly have been taken from Stratford to view the proceedings, especially the great firework display 'shewed upon the water'.

And so he may, and so he may . . .

Now, it is very quiet here. You can often, especially in winter, be quite alone and even in spring and summer, it is never at all crowded. There are seats set about on the sloping grass; children can play, climbing safely over a few low, ruined walls, or dangerously, up on the battlements. People come here to walk, sit, talk, read the daily paper, eat lunchtime sandwiches; crocodiles of schoolchildren file through the gates and then spill out in all directions, carrying worksheets attached to clip boards, chattering like parrots, and afterwards merrily picnicking on the grass beside the carefully restored Tudor stables. It is not a place where anyone need tiptoe.

The people of the present enjoy it, they rub shoulders familiarly with history, and I daresay the ghosts of the past move silently among them, and the great, handsome ruin stands sentinel over them all.

*In the chapel at Guy's Cliffe* (below), *just outside Warwick, is a large, battered statue of Guy of Warwick, the Saxon Earl, who, so the story goes, made a cave at this pretty spot and, tired of love, war and pilgrimage, here lived and died a hermit.* (Opposite) *The River Avon at Guy's Cliffe*

Warwick

You either enjoy shopping or you don't, it's a necessary chore or an agreeable pastime. But I have yet to meet anyone who fails to respond to the unique charm of shopping in an open-air market, at stalls set out, every Wednesday or Friday, Thursday or Saturday, in street or square. I'm not entirely sure *why* they are such a pleasure. It's something to do with the very fleetingness of the market – at dawn, it is deserted, an open space between silent buildings; by noon, it is a carnival of canvas awnings over barrows, wagons and trestles, a hustle and bustle of people, footsteps, the cries of the traders. At dusk, it has gone again, the marketeers have packed up their tents, and stolen away.

It all has the timeless attractiveness of a children's paper cut-out of shops, the stalls are individual and specialised – there is the cheese man, the fishmonger, the greengrocer, the man selling bowls and buckets, the one selling leather, the one selling windmills and balloons and giant pandas with neon eyes, and all those selling shirts and outsize nylon dresses, and stacks of slightly chipped china in discontinued patterns.

Shops, especially in big high streets, are all of a muchness these days – the multiple chain stores lending a disorientating sameness to towns and cities of the north, south, east and west. They're stuffy, and brightly lit and perfumed. Markets are human, cheerful, reminiscent of other times, other countries, yet uniquely English, and as alive as today.

I thought about all of this the last time we went to Warwick. It was Saturday morning and the market was in full swing. We strolled about among piled-high cauliflowers and the man shouting out the amazing virtues of a miracle potato-peeler, and it all smelled of oranges and fish and brown paper bags, and the wasps sailed about in the autumn sunshine. I couldn't think of a more enjoyable way to spend an hour, nor, offhand, of a more delightful town in which to set a market square.

*Hatton Locks, with St Mary's Church and Warwick Castle in the distance*

Quite compact, Warwick is beautiful, with some of the finest domestic architecture in the country. It isn't very large, it feels homely, and 'local', yet it has one of the biggest and most magnificent of all parish churches, and it has the castle, which draws millions of tourists every year.

Inevitably, it suffers from blocked arteries. They cannot force people to use the bypass, I suppose, and all those coaches have to get to the castle environs somehow, but if they could close off the entire area in the vicinity of the market, St Mary's Church, and the dozen or so narrow and delightful lanes and streets in and out and between, and make them pedestrian-only, it would mean a walk around the town, and life, for both residents and tourists, would be pleasanter, quieter, safer, more rewarding.

In any case, those who visit Warwick and do not penetrate this part of the town, miss a great deal – the most elegant and, in a medieval town, perhaps rather unexpected Georgian houses that lead up Church Street, the narrow lanes off the market square, and the wide and extremely handsome prospect of Northgate Street, looking up towards St Mary's.

The sight of the church tower, visible from all around, and miles away, alerts you to the importance of the whole building, but the cathedral-like height, length, and grandeur of the interior still come as a surprise.

I love St Mary's. I love the airiness of it. I love the Beauchamp chapel, with its great ornate, gilded-brass effigy of Richard, Earl of Warwick lying serenely on his high marble chest-tomb, hands raised in prayer. I love the figures of saints and angels around the east window, and the tiny Dean's chapel nearby; when you stand inside it, you seem to be surrounded by the all-white, elaborately decorated icing of some fanciful wedding cake. I love the poignant effigy of Robert Dudley, Lord Denbigh, who died in 1584, a young child, and whose small suit of armour stands in the great Hall of Warwick Castle.

Up in the nave, stand and face the chancel and the

beautiful high altar beyond, and you can imagine yourself to be in another, more solemn and religious age; sit on Sunday and listen as the voices of the choristers float upwards into the roof spaces and you are transported onto a different spiritual plane.

Walk back, down the aisle, looking towards the open doors, with the open arches of the porch, beyond them and you see, framed, the street, the cars, the busy town, going about its business of today.

And so, across to the castle, on the other side of the High Street, and I'm not quite sure where you'll find yourself. I've never known a place which is such a confusion of different ages, styles, decorations, atmosphere. Warwick Castle is everything – breathtaking, spectacular, historic, romantic, famous, exciting – and a mass of contradictions, clutter, restoration, exhibition, tourist attraction.

*Walk down the slope of Warwick High Street, away from the town, and at the far end just before the great West Gate, you come to a complex of half-timbered buildings, set around a small courtyard – the Lord Leycester Hospital.*

*The original foundation is one of the oldest in the county, once a hall belonging to two ancient Guilds, but in 1571 it became the property of Queen Elizabeth's favourite, Robert Dudley Earl of Leicester, and was converted by him into an asylum, or hospital, 'for the reception of twelve indigent men, who are called brethren'.*

*Preference was to be given to those, if any, who had been wounded or maimed in the service of their country and the statutes further say that 'every candidate must be in such circumstances of indigence as not to possess more than £5 a year on their admission. All of the members are required to wear an appropriate dress, consisting of a blue gown, with the crest of a bear and ragged staff fastened to the left sleeve; and without this badge of distinction, they are forbidden to appear in public.' Poor old men.*

*The Lord Leycester Hospital retains a great deal of its Elizabethan architecture. From the balcony, on a good day, you can see the Cotswold Hills. In the little inner courtyard, you can almost shut out the noise of the traffic grinding up the hill. There is an overhanging wooden gallery carved with odd faces and, beyond, a banqueting hall in which, if you are given a* frisson *by such touches of history, you may imagine King James I being entertained at dinner.*

(Above and opposite) *The Collegiate Church of St Mary*

*The Chapel of Our Lady – always known as the Beauchamp Chapel – is best entered not through its own doorway but down the steps that lead from the chancel so that the tomb of the Founder, Richard Beauchamp, with the golden figures set around it, is framed in the archway. It was in 1439 that the 5th Earl of Warwick completed the re-building of St Mary's, begun by his father and grandfather, and in his will he stated 'that there be made a Chapell of Our Lady, well faire and goodly built, within the middle of which Chapell I will that my Tombe be made'.*

*It is a most magnificent piece of work. Richard lies on a carved tomb-chest of marble with his gilded bronze life-size effigy on the top. He is looking up at all the company of Heaven.*

*The whole of the east wall is taken up with a glorious seven-light window, at the top of which is carved the figure of God seated in glory and holding the world in His hand. On all the panels around are saints and the nine orders of angels. On the west wall is a painting of the Last Judgment and the whole place is rich with gilded mouldings, carvings and bosses on the vaulted ceiling.*

*But to me the greatest glory of the chapel is the gallery of musical angels painted on glass in the fifteenth century. They are dancing, singing and playing instruments, and their music, a version of the song sung to the shepherds, is painted on a continuous scroll.*

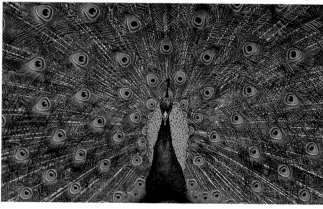

It crowns Warwick, it dominates the countryside around, and the only way to see it first, and at its most beautiful, is to approach from the lovely bridge over the Avon, Castle Bridge, and look left. And there it is – indescribable, really – one of the most painted views of any building in the world, almost as famous as Windsor Castle and, to me, more romantic, standing as it does on that craggy mound, with the gentle curve of the river below, and the lush water-meadows and shaggy trees of Warwickshire all around. It looks wonderful both at dawn and at dusk in winter, or rising out of an autumn mist when the trees are brown

(Opposite) *Guy's Tower, and* (previous page) *the view from the battlements of Guy's Tower.* (Above) *Ethelfreda's Mound from where wide open vistas towards the Cotswold Hills can be seen on clear days*

and red and gold, whether with storm clouds or azure sky behind it. Even in ordinary English rain, it doesn't lose its glory. Anyone who stands here and doesn't catch his breath at the sight has iron in his soul.

My second favourite view of it is from nearer at hand. Approach the castle by the entrance signposted off the Stratford road. There is a long, pleasantly winding drive, between bushes and shrubs and trees, and eventually the entrance through the modest, pleasingly proportioned stable block. You might be at the gateway to any rather ordinary stately home, but go through the turnstile, step out onto the path beyond, and there is the castle, green sward sweeping up to it, with the great drawbridge, the grassy moat, the mighty towers and the crenellated walls. Oddly

enough, from here, it looks smaller than you expect, more compact, but still beautiful.

Warwick Castle has the most delightful, unspoilt and, above all, spacious grounds – this is one of the most visited of all English buildings, and yet it is still possible, on the most crowded of days, to walk about the gardens, in among the trees, down over the little bridge towards the river, and feel free to breathe, without being jostled or hemmed in, as you certainly will within the keep and inside the castle itself. Everything is pleasing, but climb to the top of the newly opened mound, and you can feel like a bird perched in a tree, master of the whole of the county, and of wide open vistas towards the Cotswold Hills. And in June, the rose garden, restored to all its former glory and replanted according to plans discovered in the county archives, is utterly English; blowsy, extravagant, almost, but not quite, too much. It has rose arches, rose arbours, rose walks – tumbling, cascading, climbing, rambling, over-branching roses; the effect is extraordinarily lush, and heavily scented as Daisy, Countess of Warwick's boudoir.

I really don't know what to make of the interior of Warwick Castle. I think I'd rather not go in at all. From all the space and massive, imposing, dominating grandeur of the building, you step into half-a-dozen different periods and styles, all leading in and out of one another – medieval, Elizabethan, Regency, Victorian, Edwardian. There is armour and there are damask-hung walls, and a curiously un-spooky ghost tower, there is gilding and ornamentation, there are tapestried beds and over-stuffed sofas, festoon blinds and spectacularly ugly pieces of furniture. There are also some extraordinary waxwork tableaux of the domestic interior of the castle during a weekend houseparty in the Edwardian era, and I found them, as I always find waxworks, inexplicably creepy – far more so than any ghost room. They are, however, much prized, much admired, much visited, and the whole display has won all manner of awards as a tourist attraction, which must please the new owners of Warwick Castle – for in 1982 the present Earl sold the whole place, lock, stock and barrel, to Madame Tussauds.

But what does that matter if they care for the place, repair the fabric, restore what has been neglected, as well as they obviously do? Look at any of the marvellous paintings of the place that hang on the walls – and there are plenty, because the owners are trying to buy back for the castle as many pictures as possible. And then, still marvelling, go back to Castle Bridge, and look again at the reality. Nothing has gone, nothing has been lost. There it is before you, the same castle, the same river Avon, the same lovely fields and trees that have inspired and uplifted so many great artists and writers, visitors from every country in the world, ordinary citizens of Warwickshire. Somehow it is one of those sights, like Venice, that you can never take for granted.

*Warwick Castle from the river*

From Edge Hill

I went to live in Royal Leamington Spa in 1968, for no other reason than because I liked it. That is the great advantage of being single and a self-employed writer, able to settle where the fancy takes you, not constrained by family or job. I liked its broad, elegant avenues, its public park with sober gravelled walk, formal flower-beds, and pretty fountains spouting from the little lake. I liked its shops – in those days rather smarter than they have since become – its Italianate villas, and Regency crescents of white stuccoed houses. Leamington Spa reminded me of Scarborough where I was born, of Southport and Harrogate, where I spent many a childhood holiday, of Bath, which I had later come to admire. And there is a character to all the English spa towns that is an amalgam of a gracious past, with fine architecture and a spacious layout, that I find particularly congenial.

Leamington has changed, of course, and not entirely for the better. Nowhere can exist on nostalgia, and I do not want time to stand still so that living places stagnate, or become fossilised and dead – like those immaculately preserved villages of Laycock or Castle Combe. Towns are where people live and work, they change because life changes, fortunes fluctuate, populations grow. Leamington Spa has grown much larger, light (and some heavier) industry has flourished on its margins, it has a large immigrant population; it seems to have grown in spirit closer to the West Midlands than to the Shakespeare country. The quality shops have given way to the popular chains, and a large

*Lansdowne Circus, Leamington Spa*

number of students has moved in, using the town as a residential outpost of the University of Warwick, bringing a new sort of vitality and style to the place, along with wholefood shops, fringe theatre, and left-wing graffiti.

As the old, retired genteel ladies of John Betjeman's melancholy poem have died, so, alas, their handsome villas have often not only been sold, but demolished, to be replaced by hideous blocks of flats. I saw a good many of those four-square dwellings disappear when I lived in the town, and it has lost a good many more since – so that Pevsner's claim in *The Buildings of England*, that 'the pride of Leamington Spa is its villas', no longer holds quite true.

But the River Leam is still there, and the bridges over it, the parks and gardens and all those beautiful trees, and streets wide enough to accommodate horse-drawn carriages are quite able to cope with even today's quantity of motor cars.

Because my time was my own to organise as I chose, so long as I did enough work to earn a living, and because I used to write in exhausting bursts, and then lie fallow for weeks on end, I was able to wander fairly freely, not only within the town, but out of it. I drove my noisy little grey mini-van almost every afternoon, to explore miles of the countryside around Leamington, and over towards Warwick and Stratford, Banbury, Shipston-on-Stour, and down as far as Oxford. I went in all seasons, all weathers, but because I could choose my times, I went most often in early spring before the tourists had arrived, or in late autumn and winter when they had left. I avoided weekends, and main roads. I meandered, without so much as a map, following signposts in all directions, discovering.

And in that way I came by chance upon so many places, well-known and unknown, and felt all the excitement of the treasure-seeker who has found the hidden gold all for himself. Sometimes I would return home to look up the village, house or view on the map and in the guide-book, and realise that, quite inadvertently, I had gone to the most famous place in the area.

At other times, my find would be obscure, some sleepy hamlet right off the beaten track, apparently known only to its inhabitants.

They were the happiest of days. I was always alone, which is the best condition for serious looking and taking-in, one is not distracted at all by companionship and conversation, so that those times, what I saw and felt about it all are vivid in my memory still, and in detail rather than in general.

And perhaps more clearly than any other day, I remember the one when I came quite by chance upon what still seems to me the most magical house I have ever seen, quite perfect in its setting, a place I visited, after that first time, as often as I could and which has still not lost its importance to me.

It was in the autumn, early October I think, one of those rare, golden afternoons when the sun is hot and the sky blue, and yet there is the unmistakable smell of the year's turn in the air. The hedges were thick with blackberries, rowan berries red as blood, and dark, dark sloes, the corn was long cut, and most of the earth was brown again, and here and there, a hayrick, or a stack of bales, stood, dark yellow. All the gardens of the villages I went through had trees bent with fruit and wigwams of runner beans that had been pinched and blackened at the tips by the previous night's frost. There were thin blue plumes of smoke spiralling upwards, and wasps everywhere.

I drove through winding, quite narrow lanes, between low hedges, looking across the fields of Warwickshire, to the clumps and lines and thickets of trees whose leaves were all the colours of red and brown and gold, up slopes, down slopes, along the flat, I was going nowhere in particular. I turned left, because I thought I would, climbed a steeper hill, and came among some thicker, darker trees. At the top, seeing a sign to a house, I stopped the van in a clearing, got out and walked a few yards to where there was a wide gap in the trees, and looked down.

There, below me, in a bowl surrounded by grassy slopes, was the most beautiful house I had ever seen.

Because it was such a complete surprise and was sitting there in the autumn sunshine so unexpectedly, I blinked, and looked again, and half-expected it to have suddenly vanished. It was the house of enchantment, and of fairy stories, and yet not some fantasy castle, but a mellow, many-chimneyed Elizabethan manor, set among lawns, rose beds and ornamental ponds, with the tree-dotted basin of green rising gently up on all sides of it, and a long broad drive down to it. It was built of so many soft tints of brick, all blending together, rose-red, geranium red, dark brown, yellow-grey, grey-black.

I stood, and stared, and stared at the beautiful house, with the beautiful name to match that I had read on a sign-board, Compton Wynyates.

That day, the house itself was closed to visitors but the grounds were open, and there was no one else about. I bought my ticket at the little wooden hut, and went to wander around and, eventually, just to sit, up on the grassy slope in company with some sheep, and bask in the late afternoon sun, and smell the autumn air, and gaze and gaze.

After that, I went to Compton Wynyates again and again, as soon as it re-opened the following spring. I was never tired of the beauty of it, it seemed such an unimposing, unpretentiously beautiful house. I took a book and papers, and read or worked, sitting on the slopes. I sat in my van, in the clearing off the lane looking down on it, and ate my sandwiches. I went into the house when it was open but, oddly enough, I remember very little about it except a priest's hole somewhere. I have always cared far more for the exteriors of such places, and the rooms of so many of them, the oak and the portraits and the tapestried sofas, all blend together into one historic interior in my mind.

For three years, I haunted Compton Wynyates. I went there, always alone, on fair days and on grey

(Previous page) *Compton Wynyates, the most beautiful house I had ever seen.* (Right) *From the top of Edge Hill*

days, in warm sunshine and in cold winds, to wander about, to sit in the garden or on the grassy slopes, with a book or my thoughts, but mostly, just to look and look.

Then for the following fifteen years, I was haunted *by* it, as I am by so many places of the past. It was hidden deep in the thicket of memory; I did not visit it again, only knew that it would be there for me, when I wanted it.

Sometimes it had been very quiet when I went there; more often, and especially at weekends and holidays – which I soon learned to avoid – it was crowded, there were coaches and cars advancing up and backing down the steep and narrow surrounding lanes, people thronging the gardens, and shuffling after the guides around the beautiful house. As with every other such property, you had to pick your times, go early or late in the season, or at the very beginning of the week, to be sure of having peace there, of being almost completely alone.

So when at last I visited it again, one late August Sunday in 1986, I was surprised that the lanes were completely deserted, no coaches, not another single car – through the little villages – turn left – up the hill between the trees. No one. I came to the small clearing by the gates at the head of the drive, and got out. Everything was quite quiet, quite still. And there was Compton Wynyates, as beautiful as ever, nestling in its green bowl below. There were the barley-sugar chimneys and the bricks, in soft tints like the walls and roofs of some sunlit Italian village, the immaculate lawn and the rougher grassy slopes, the glimpse of the shining pools, the last of the rambling roses. Oh, most beautiful of houses.

And there, beside me, the reason why Compton Wynyates stood, all to itself, and everything was quiet. Two large notice boards inform that the house and grounds 'are no longer open to the public'.

For a moment, I felt so sad, so frustrated. I could have cried. But gradually, as I walked slowly up the lane, and along the top path under the trees, catching a glimpse of the house below through gaps in the hedges, losing it, seeing it again, I felt something else. Because it is no longer open and accessible to all, Compton Wynyates has become a mysterious, tantalising, magical place.

I felt like someone forever condemned to remain outside a paradise, looking in at a house of dreams and visions and fairy tales, which I could invest with all manner of attributes that in reality I knew it did not have, or like Alice, when she knelt down and looked along the passage into 'the loveliest garden you ever saw. How she longed to get out of that dark hall, and wander about among those beds of bright flowers, and those cool fountains'.

But I realised that I did not. The best of Compton Wynyates is its exterior, and you can see that as well – or better – from the clearing above as by being close to it, and the fact that it is private now, and entrance is forbidden, lends it a tremendous enchantment.

And I'm glad that the house is lived in, not a museum, full of red ropes and loquacious guides, but a home, with meals cooked in the kitchens and eaten in the dining hall, and beds that are slept in, with dogs and cats and real smoke coming up through those glorious chimneys.

I came away, gladdened by the sight of it, again soothed in the silence, feeling that such places ought to guard their privacy and retain their mystery more often.

The area across from Compton Wynyates, east, towards Edge Hill and its surrounding villages, is one of the loveliest, and least known, in Warwickshire. The main roads, from Stratford and Warwick to Banbury, are narrow, and busy with too heavy a volume of traffic, but all the minor roads and lanes that criss-cross between are relatively quiet. This is a land of little rises and curves; of slopes and low ridges swathed in clumps of broad-leaved woodland, of sunny fields with little rivulets running through – tiny tributaries of the Dene. There are numerous very small, sleepy hamlets, some on the flat, others high up and hanging on the edge of the escarpment and, as you go by, you often see those four-square, modestly handsome houses – the old vicarages, rectories and manors of England, well-kept, well-loved, well-surrounded by gardens and pretty cottages. Every parish church has something worth seeing – the lovely steeple of St John the Baptist at Avon Dassett, set on the steep hillside; the statue of a Royalist captain, killed at the battle of Edge Hill, at Radway – though there is only one, at Burton Dassett, which is truly extraordinary.

I love this countryside, it doesn't shout about itself.

You could easily pass it by, and it has a very particular, haunted atmosphere.

Haunted, more than anywhere else, of course, at Edge Hill itself where that famous, bloody battle between Cavaliers and Roundheads was fought nearly 350 years ago. You need to come up here in winter, on one of the bleak, bitter afternoons of December or January when the wind whistles and moans across the dark fields and uphill through the bare trees, into your face. The sky scuds with lowering clouds, and there is

*May on Edge Hill*

no one at all about. Then, if you stand on the very edge of Edge Hill, and look down, you can, if you half-close your eyes, see the steely armies, hear the groans of dying men, and the whinnicking of terrified horses; as you look across the empty countryside, there are spectacular views, and it's a sinister place. But in summer, you could simply miss it, driving on the road past an ugly pub, set in a tower where the hedges and trees are too dense to allow you more than a glimpse of the land that stretches away below. Battlefields are the most moving of places, even though there is nothing left to see but ploughed earth and little hedges. I never know whether or not I truly do believe in ghosts – but I *think* that I do, and certainly I believe in haunted places which make you feel suddenly very cold, very afraid, very alone – and yet not alone. The countryside around Edge Hill does that.

If you want to know more, about the ghosts of Edge Hill and the battle itself, how they formed up, what they wore, who led, who died, who won, you can find it out at the new small, war museum in a lovely converted barn, set in the grounds of Farnborough Hall. It's a shoe-string enterprise run by enthusiasts, full of interest, and not for one moment dull, but exactly the kind of place that 'brings history alive'. Worth making a special pilgrimage to.

*Sheep country*

But then so is the Hall itself, another of those unexpected gems, hidden away in the middle of the English countryside, far more pleasing than many a more famous place on the well-beaten tourist route. It isn't very large at all, nor open too often, and one of the delights of the house is that it is actually lived in. When you go to look round, therefore, you find the ashes of last night's log fire in the grate, and the smell of today's dinner wafting through from the back regions, and a wooden duck on wheels under a marble table. It is a seventeenth-century house, square, elegant, sober on the outside and ridiculously ornamented within, like a frivolous, marvellous wedding cake of plaster-work, swags and wreaths, flowers and fruit, ribbons and roses, ornate, unnecessary, breathtaking. I don't suppose anyone living now could do work like it, nor how much it would cost, but if there were and I were a millionaire, I should want a house decorated with plasterwork in the style of Farnborough.

(Above) *Farnborough Hall and* (opposite) *the view from the terrace*

And who could not stand at the front door and look at the prospect it frames, and not feel better? There is a gateway with trees beyond, a long, straight drive leading between stone arches up to a perfectly circular lawn. Nothing incongruous or superfluous at all to spoil the line of it.

But the pride of Farnborough, aside from the plasterwork, is its setting. It is surrounded by some of the proudest, mightiest trees I have ever seen; graceful groups set around and beside a series of small artificially-made lakes – including, since this is a ghostly part of the country, one haunted by a lady in white.

Walk out onto the lawn at the back of the house, turn left. From here, for three-quarters of a mile, you are on the terrace walk, laid out on the ridge overlooking the Warwickshire Plain and for miles away, away,

looking towards the Malverns. It looks an easy, natural piece of landscaping, with a broad grass walk set with a border of laurel hedges, and trees behind, and here and there, set about with an Ionic temple, an oval pavilion, an alcove, an obelisk. But like all apparently effortless, simple works of art, it would have taken not only a landscape garden designer of rare vision – in this case William Holbech – but an enormous amount of hard labour, skilled as well as unskilled. It is a triumph, exhilarating, spacious, gracious, fun, one of the best planned walks in the country.

Take it while you can. Go to Farnborough Hall and bask in the uninterrupted views from the terrace walk. Let your eye enjoy the fields, the trees, the hedges, the line of the river, as far as you can see. Stand and listen to the silence – for even on a busy day in summer, this is an extraordinarily quiet spot. I imagine that, on grey, wet afternoons in November, it is gloomy too; the trees will drip, drip, drip in the silence, the air will scarcely stir.

Not for much longer. In the National Trust booklet that describes Farnborough Hall, there is a fine photograph of the view from the terrace. It was taken in 1954, but had scarcely changed in 1986. Underneath this photograph is the single sentence: 'The M40 motorway will bisect this valley.'

So that view, that great stretch of plain, of field and tree and meadow, that peace and curious air of isolation and old-fashionedness that are the joys of Farnborough Hall, are doomed to death.

In the autumn of 1969, some friends who were going abroad asked me if I would look after their dog for three months. He was a Jack Russell terrier, small and supple and neat, and clever as paint, with a cocked ear and a black eye patch. His name was Nip.

In those days, I lived alone, with my cat Hastings for company, and I was uncertain how a dog would suit the household, but when he arrived, he very intelligently decided that the safest course would be to let the cat continue to rule the roost, while he fitted into the small corners. But there was always an uneasy truce between them, and I could often feel Nip quivering with the suppressed desire for the chase and because he was also generally very energetic, I took him out as much as possible. We walked the streets of Leamington Spa, and combed every inch of its parks, both early and late, but I sensed that this was not what Nip really wanted. He needed wide open spaces and rabbit holes, and I was in despair of finding either without taking him on a moorland holiday when I mentioned the problem to a neighbour. 'Well, don't you know where to go?' he asked in amazement. 'You want to take him to the Dassett Hills. That'd be his paradise.'

For the next three months, until just before Christmas, they became mine, too.

When Bob mentioned them, I didn't dare confess that I'd never *heard* of the Dassett Hills, let alone knew where they were.

I went out and bought a map.

There are plenty of signposts to them now, and the area has been re-designated Burton Dassett Country Park. People hang-glide from off the top of them on Sunday afternoons, and race bicycles madly up and down the little switchback roads. But in those days, nobody much seemed to know about them, or go there, except locals and a few children flying kites, and the first time I went, with the dog Nip, they were completely deserted. I might have been on Dartmoor,

*The Burton Dassett Hills*

*All Saints church, Burton Dassett*

or the wide open hills of Cumbria, they felt so remote, so bare and, by comparison with all the vale below, so high.

The Dassett Hills are reached south-east out of Warwick via Gaydon, or Stratford-upon-Avon, going east, through Kineton in the direction of the villages of Northend and Fenny Compton. Then Avon Dassett, which climbs with the hill, is signposted, and the road narrows until, quite unexpectedly, you are up on the Hills.

They don't cover a very wide area, and they are set above quite neat and pretty and refined villages, often inhabited by commuters from Warwick and Leamington Spa and even Banbury, with roses-round-the-door cottages interspersed with modern bungalows. This is pleasant, quiet, undramatic countryside, nice, but rather tame. But it's also very close to Edge Hill, and up at Burton Dassett itself, the air is quite different, the wind blows cold, and there are ghosts about.

That first afternoon, I parked my van in a gateway, got out with Nip, and looked all around these rolling humps of ancient grassland under the wild, scudding sky, filled with delight at such a place, astonished by it. There are no trees, only the chalky, beautifully rounded hummocks, with a narrow track across them, and the melancholy bleating of sheep from all around. Nip found his rabbit holes and vanished, and I stood, on the top of the highest hill, and felt the earth spin. It was a grey, wild afternoon, and I could see for miles, the whole of Warwickshire laid out at my feet, and to the north, the rooftops of the small town of Southam, with the tall chimney of a cement works there. Suddenly the clouds broke apart, and just for a few seconds, the sun lanced through and lit up a band of the country, taking in the chimney and picking out the plume of smoke from it, setting it on fire. The whole scene, all light and dark and heavy sky, was like a John Martin oil painting. Then, it was gone, the clouds closed in, and the wind almost blew me over.

Because I was born in wilder country, where it is higher, colder, barer, I always long for such places and have to find them where I can. On the Dassett Hills, I felt at home and, exhilarated, I ran up and down with Nip at my heels, all the cobwebs and stuffiness of the river valley blowing away on the wind.

Nip had had a wonderful time, but he was the most obedient of dogs and returned at once to the van when I whistled, leaped in to the back, curled like a cat, nose to stumpy tail, and went to sleep. I left him there and walked a hundred yards on down the track, to see if there was anything else to see before setting off for home. On the map, there was a church. I like churches. Perhaps it would be interesting.

And so, almost by accident, I found All Saints, Burton Dassett, one of the most amazing, and historic and perfect small churches in the entire country, unspoilt, silent, peaceful, so full of the past you feel you could walk up to the chancel and walk back into it. Yet it is not dead, or uncared for, it is a church full of the worship and prayers and life of the present, too.

It lies in a shallow bowl, with a house or two nearby but not crowding it in, surrounded by grass, and sheep and trees, and the most wonderful of graveyards set on a slope, and with views for miles over the meadows and hedgerows.

Outside, it is sturdy, stone and four-square, with a flat-topped tower. Good, plain, wholesome. But the inside takes your breath away. It is absolutely plain with whitewashed walls, and it slopes uphill at the chancel end. It is full of light and air and silence, but although the lines are austere, there is decoration of the most beautiful kind, a half-revealed, half-hidden wall painting over the chancel arch, a passion, with a virgin of wide-eyes emerging from her shadowy robe, and hints here and there of an angel, a cross, but all faint, faded, almost washed out.

And around the capitals of the pillars are stone carvings like those in the Romanesque churches of southern France; real animals, rabbits, snakes, a lamb, all chasing one another's tails, round and round and round; there is a mythical beast and all is set among delicately carved foliage. Near the roof on the corbel-stones, the sculptor has chiselled faces, but not hideous gargoyles – they look real, the faces of the local countrymen of four hundred years ago.

This is one of the most peaceful places I know. When you go outside, you hear nothing but sheep, birds, occasionally the drone of a distant plane, the whine of the wind. Inside the church, the air seethes and presses into your ears like the sound of the sea inside a seashell.

Yet it was not always so. This is Civil War country. The noise of bloody battle at Edge Hill must have swirled around this quiet place and the chancel arch is riddled with shot, probably from the guns of Round-heads attacking the Royal Arms which were painted here. Nor was it always so deserted, with the church standing alone among the sheep and the gravestones.

Once, a whole row of cottages ran in a line from the church, people lived here, and cultivated their garden plots. Now it is corn which is so profitable that men have ripped out hedgerows and ancient woodlands and changed the face of the countryside in pursuit of open land on which it will grow. In medieval England, it was sheep, whose wool made so many merchants rich, which gobbled up the land. On the Burton Dassett Hills, farmers and cottagers were turned out and their dwellings razed, so that the acres could be enclosed for sheep rearing. The countryside never recovered from that depopulation.

When I used to go there, day after day, with the dog Nip, I felt grateful for the place, its quietness, and emptiness, and the cries of the sheep, but sad, too, affected by the past in a way I seldom am. It was a cold, grey autumn that year, the trees were soon bare and there were no golden days of late sunshine. I walked the Dassett Hills in bleak winds, and always the sky seemed to be huge and racing with clouds, always the sheep sounded like crying human voices down the wind. A place of ghosts, yes.

It hasn't changed really, in spite of the kites and bicycles and men trying to be birds on Saturdays and Sundays, in spite of being called 'a country park'. The church is still as quiet, light, and gravely beautiful, the sheep still cry, the people still sleep peacefully under that ancient earth.

We took our younger daughter there, when she had just learned to walk. She stumbled intently, seriously, up and down the nave of the church and, outside, in the grass among the graves, finding a ladybird on a stone, seeing a butterfly, making little exclamations of interest and delight. Young life in an ancient place.

*The interior of All Saints church.* (Overleaf) *Sun Rising Hill, looking towards the Malverns*

# Upton House

This corner of Warwickshire, nowhere near so well-known and well-visited as the areas around Stratford and Warwick, contains some of the best villages, the best churches, the most beautiful countryside and, above all, the finest prospects, of the whole country. Within a few square miles, you find the Dassett Hills, Edge Hill and the spectacular Sun Rising Hill and, nearby, three of what must surely be the handsomest houses in England. Compton Wynyates will always be closest to my heart, the flower of them all; Farnborough Hall is the most compact and decorative, its terrace walk commanding the best views over the open countryside. Then about four miles south-west of Farnborough, set back off the Stratford to Banbury road, is Upton House.

Upton is handsome, finely proportioned, elegant from the other side of the valley, especially at night when the lights in the house are switched on and it looks like a mighty liner becalmed between waves. The grounds are extensive and panoramic, the trees mature and graceful, and when you reach the edge of the lawn, you look down a series of stepped terraces onto what almost seems to me the pride of the place, a south-facing, sheltered kitchen garden whose lovely, orderly rows of peas and beans, currant bushes and corn cobs, carrots and cabbages, ought to convince anyone that vegetables, when properly grown, are objects of beauty, as worthy to be admired as the most carefully cultivated herbaceous borders.

Step down to this level, and the air feels several degrees warmer. You cannot see the house or the lawn, they are obscured by the rising bank. Here you can stroll along shady paths sloping this way and that between the trees, or walk to what is rather unappealingly called the Bog Garden, a delightful, almost Japanese water-garden, with little bridges and stepping stones over rivulets coming from a central pool, rich in plants that thrive in such damp, low, marshy places.

But if a walk in the gardens, and an admiring sight of the long façade of the house are among the pleasures of a visit to Upton, they are not the principal reason for coming here, for the real riches of the house are hidden away inside. It contains, in rooms especially altered and re-designed to show them off, one of the most magnificent collections of porcelain and paintings to be found outside a museum in this country. For once, it is the interior of the house and what it contains as much as the grounds, which will bring me back time after time.

I first learned to enjoy looking at pictures when I was a very small child, taken to the local art gallery on Sunday afternoons by my mother. I might have found it all very tedious but somehow I did not. The pictures were probably not all of very fine quality, but I began to understand, simply by looking, which were the best and which I liked. Later, I learned more when I was lent books on Italian, Dutch and British painting by a generous and enthusiastic art mistress at school. When I went up to university, I had the good fortune to live very near to the V & A which I could drop into for a few minutes almost every day, and I spent a good deal of time in the National Gallery, too. Looking at pictures has been one of the best pleasures and deepest enrichments of my life, and I discovered that it teaches you to look with new eyes at everything *else* – the landscape, gardens, houses, furnishings, objects, artefacts – the vision of great painters flows out of their work and touches the whole of life.

And at Upton, there are some of the most breath-taking pictures I have ever seen. You come upon some of them almost accidentally – a Constable, unmistakable with its grey sky, watery light and Suffolk fields, hangs just by a doorway as you enter one of the sitting rooms, a rather famous, large oil of the park at Upton House in the late eighteenth century, painted by Anthony Devis, the sky is like an eggshell, the bare trees delicate as lace, and there are three men, perfectly posed, skating elegantly on the frozen lake. It is a magical scene.

There is Stubbs, there is Gainsborough, there is a

*The terraced herbaceous border*

mighty, brooding small landscape by Ruisdael, which might well be another Constable, and a cool, formal, strangely modern interior of Utrecht cathedral by Saenredam which repays not close but distant viewing, from a few yards down the long room when it reveals its depths, and careful patterning.

All of these are housed upstairs, in 'real' rooms, with views of the park beyond the tall windows. Downstairs are two specially designed small galleries, with good overhead light, crammed with astonishing treasures. Your eyes pop out as you move from a Rembrandt to a Giotto, to a Brueghel to an El Greco, with pages from illuminated manuscripts, psalters, Books of Hours standing open on small easels in between them all. The centrepiece is a nativity triptych, by Bosch, set almost modestly there, taking its place among all the other masterpieces, and so beautiful it makes you want to kneel down.

There is almost too much in a small space, you need to come often, to stand in front of just a few paintings at a time, and to enjoy the porcelain, too, principally Chelsea and Sèvres. This was collected, like the pictures, rather quickly between the two world wars, by the 2nd Viscount Bearsted. He must have been a remarkable man.

Coming out of the front door and looking up the long, straight, immaculate drive that leads to the main road and so away into Warwickshire, you feel a curious sense of unreality. Among so many amazing pictures, you lose not only all sense of time, but any sense of place, too. Then, suddenly, there you are again, walking out between English oaks and chestnuts and beeches, towards a gravel car park and, behind you, and behind that heavy oak door, the calm portraits of gracious ladies and the solemn Virgin and adoring angels, the huntsmen for ever galloping across eighteenth-century landscapes, the Suffolk cottages and the Dutch canals, inhabit another world, silent, still, immortal.

*Sun Rising Hill*

Postscript

Some of the beauties of the Shakespeare country are obvious and well known. Some places are over-rated and over-crowded. I like the area for my own, highly personal reasons, but I like it too because it has so many hidden – even secret – delights; tucked away corners, little known villages, and sudden spectacular vistas which are all the more precious set in a part of the country so famous and well trodden. The best is off the beaten track – perhaps that is true of any tourist area. If you want peace and a chance to get to know the particular charms of both the countryside and town and village, you have to make an effort. You will be rewarded a hundredfold.

As I visited Shakespeare country again in the course of writing this book, I have been wondering which bits I should long for most if I were to be forcibly prevented from ever going there again. They would mostly be views from a distance, buildings or villages set in a frame of the countryside – Chipping Campden, seen from the high hills around; Warwick Castle, mighty on its mound, seen from the bridge across the Avon; the church of Holy Trinity at Stratford with the river flowing behind it; Kenilworth Castle, set against a blood-red sky. And, more than anywhere else, Compton Wynyates, glimpsed below, through its shelter of trees.

There are places I have not mentioned. The tiny,

(Below) *Mill on the River Stour.* (Previous page) *The Avon at Ashow and* (opposite) *at Welford-on-Avon*

(Opposite and above) *The church of St Mary at Halford.*
(Overleaf) *Tredington church*

almost too picturesque village of Ashow, near Stoneleigh, quiet among fields and trees and trickling water, perfect Warwickshire. Tredington church spire, one of the most elegant in the county. The exquisite Romanesque carvings on the tympanum above the door of Halford church. The market square of Shipston-on-Stour, plain, honest, homely, pleasing.

Shakespeare country is changing, nowhere is really safe from the invasion of new roads, greater volume of traffic, encroaching housing development. Stratford desperately needs a second river crossing, Henley-in-Arden a by-pass. When they get them, more green fields and quiet backwater lanes will be gobbled up. The extension of the M40 from London to Birmingham will slash across the little known, quietly beautiful Warmington Valley, and places like Farnborough Hall and the villages surrounding Edge Hill will never be the same again. As more and more commuters come to live in the M40 corridor, so they will grow.

This is an area of growth, every year it *feels* closer to the industrial Midlands. Every month it seems Stratford gets more crowded with tourists and their traffic, a once quiet area of the town is opened up for housing and, in the process, the character of the place is irrevocably altered. You will have to search even harder to find any real Shakespeare country.

In a way I feel I have almost been catching the past, my own and that of these places, as it flies. Everything has been changing as I have written. In twenty years' time, I wonder how much of what I have so described will remain and be recognisable. I am only grateful to have lived in the Shakespeare country and to have got to know it so intimately in these past happy years.

# Selected Properties

*THE NATIONAL TRUST*
Regional Information Office
The National Trust
Severn Regional Office
34-36 Church Street
Tewkesbury
Gloucestershire
GL20 5SN

Telephone: (0684) 292919 & 292427 & 297747

*Baddesley Clinton*
Baddesley Clinton
Knowle
Solihull
B93 0DQ

Telephone: (05643) 3294

Open: April to end September, Wednesday
     to Sunday;
     October, Saturday and Sunday.
Closed: Good Friday.

*Coughton Court*
Coughton Court
nr. Alcester
Warwickshire
B49 5JA

Telephone: (0789) 762435

Open: May to end September except Monday and
     Friday.
     April and October open Saturday and Sunday.

*Farnborough Hall*
Farnborough Hall
Banbury
Oxfordshire
OX17 1DZ
Open: April to end September, Wednesday
     and Saturday.
     Terrace Walk: Thursday, Friday and
     Sunday.

*The Fleece Inn*
The Fleece Inn
Bretforton
nr. Evesham
Worcestershire

Telephone: (0386) 831173

Open normal public house licensing hours
throughout year.

*Hidcote Manor Garden*
Hidcote Manor Garden
Hidcote Bartrim
nr. Chipping Campden
Gloucestershire
GL55 6LR

Telephone: (038677) 333

Open: Easter Saturday to end October.
Closed: Tuesday and Friday.

*Packwood House*
Packwood House
Lapworth
Solihull
B94 6AT

Telephone: (05643) 2024

Open: April to end September, Wednesday
     to Sunday.
     October: Saturday and Sunday.

*Upton House*
Upton House
nr. Banbury
Oxfordshire
OX15 6HT

Telephone: The Estate Office: (029587) 266

Open: April to end September, Monday to Thursday
    also certain Saturdays and Sundays in May,
    July, and August.


*THE SHAKESPEARE BIRTHPLACE TRUST*

*Administrative Headquarters*
The Shakespeare Birthplace Trust
The Shakespeare Centre
Stratford-upon-Avon
CV37 6QW

Telephone: (0789) 204016

*Anne Hathaway's Cottage*
Anne Hathaway's Cottage
Shottery
Stratford-upon-Avon
Warwickshire

Telephone: (0789) 292100

Open throughout the year except Christmas Eve,
    Christmas Day and Boxing Day.

*Birthplace*
Birthplace
Henley Street
Stratford-upon-Avon
Warwickshire

Telephone: (0789) 204016

Open throughout the year except Christmas Eve,
    Christmas Day and Boxing Day.

*Hall's Croft*
Hall's Croft
Old Town
Stratford-upon-Avon
Warwickshire

Telephone (0789) 292107

Open throughout the year.
Closed: Sundays from November to March and
    Christmas Eve, Christmas Day and
    Boxing Day.

*Mary Arden's House*
Mary Arden's House
Wilmcote
Stratford-upon-Avon
Warwickshire

Telephone: (0789) 293455

Open throughout the year.
Closed: Sundays from November to March and
    Christmas Eve, Christmas Day and
    Boxing Day.

*New Place & Nash's House*
New Place
Chapel Street
Stratford-upon-Avon
Warwickshire

Telephone: (0789) 292325

Open throughout the year.
Closed: Sundays from November to March and
    Christmas Eve, Christmas Day and
    Boxing Day.

## STRATFORD-UPON-AVON

### Tourist Information Office
1 High Street
Stratford-upon-Avon
Warwickshire
CV37 6AU

Telephone: (0789) 293127

### King Edward VI Grammar School
King Edward VI Grammar School
Church Street
Stratford-upon-Avon
Warwickshire
CV37 6HB

Telephone: (0789) 293351

Open occasionally during school holidays.

### Guild Chapel
Guild Chapel
Chapel Lane
Stratford-upon-Avon
Warwickshire

Open throughout the year.

### Holy Trinity Church
Holy Trinity Church
Old Town
Stratford-upon-Avon
Warwickshire

Telephone: Parish Office: (0789) 66316

Open throughout the year.

### Royal Shakespeare Theatre, Swan Theatre, & The Other Place
For all bookings telephone: (0789) 295623
24 hour booking information: (0789) 69191

Season: end March to end January.

## WARWICK

### Tourist Information Office
The Court House
Jury Street
Warwick

Telephone: (0926) 492212

### Warwick Castle
Warwick Castle
Warwick
CV34 4QU

Telephone: (0926) 495421

Open every day (except Christmas Day).

### Lord Leycester Hospital
Lord Leycester Hospital
Warwick
CV34 4BH

Telephone: (0926) 491422 & 492797

Open throughout the year except Sundays, Good Friday, and Christmas Day.

### St Mary's Church
St Mary's Vicarage
The Butts
Warwick
CV34 4SS

Telephone: Parish Office (0926) 491132

Open throughout the year.

## MISCELLANEOUS

### Charlecote Park
Charlecote Park
Wellesbourne
Warwickshire
CV35 9ER

Telephone: (0789) 840277

Open: May to end September except Mondays and
Thursdays. April and October open Saturdays
and Sundays.

### Compton Wynyates
Compton Wynyates
Tysoe
Warwickshire

No longer open to public. Visitors by
appointment only.

### Kenilworth Castle
Kenilworth Castle
Kenilworth
Warwickshire

Open throughout the year except Christmas and
New Year's Day.

### Ragley Hall
Ragley Hall
Alcester
Warwickshire

Telephone: (0789) 762090 & 762455

House and Park: Open April to end September.
(House only: Closed Mondays and Fridays
except for Bank Holiday Mondays.)

# Photographic Acknowledgements

Robin Whiteman and Rob Talbot would like to thank everyone who so willingly gave their time to guide them around the properties and sites. They particularly wish to acknowledge the generous co-operation they received from the National Trust (Severn Region), The Shakespeare Birthplace Trust, and Warwick Castle in allowing them unrestricted access to their properties over an entire year.

They are also grateful to the following: the Marquess of Hertford (Ragley Hall); Captain E. H. Lee RN and the Governors of Lord Leycester Hospital (Warwick); Nicola Russell (Royal Shakespeare Company); Mr N. W. R. Mellon, Headmaster of King Edward VI Grammar School; Mr P. F. Latham, Town Clerk of Stratford-upon-Avon Town Council; the Warwickshire Constabulary at Stratford-upon-Avon; The Rector and the Churchwardens of the Collegiate Church of Holy Trinity (Stratford-upon-Avon); The Rector and the Churchwardens of the Collegiate Church of St Mary the Virgin (Warwick); Joseph E. Tilley and family for access to Chesterton Woods.

Special thanks go to: Dr Levi Fox, Director of The Shakespeare Birthplace Trust, Miss Barbara Morley, Regional Information Officer of the National Trust (Severn Region), and Jennie Davies, formerly of Michael Joseph Ltd; appreciation goes also to all those individuals too numerous to mention by name who nevertheless made such a valuable contribution.

pages 2–3: *Windmill Hill near Compton Wynyates*
pages 4–5: *Looking east towards Stratford*
pages 6–7: *Near Wilmcote*
this page: *Broadway Tower*
page 192: *Chesterton windmill*

# Index

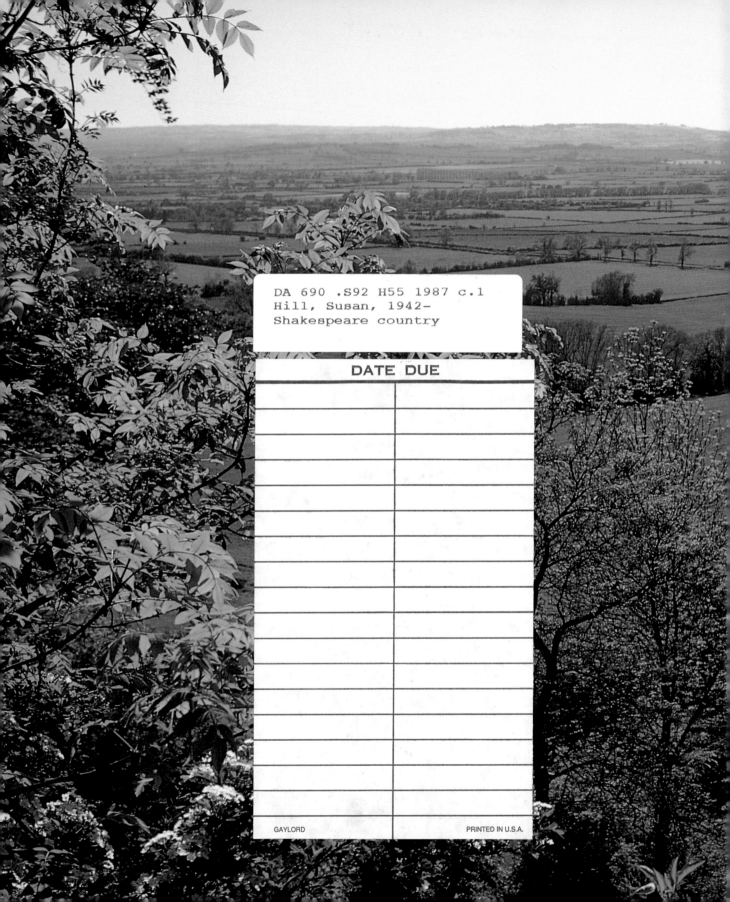